Chronic Fatigue

and the

Great Cycle of Life

Chronic Fatigue and the Great Cycle of Life

DC Lynch

Great Cycle Press

Coos Bay, Oregon, USA

First Edition

Great Cycle Press

Coos Bay, Oregon

ISBN: 979-8-9871177-0-5

Library of Congress Control Number: 2022919463

Manufactured in the United States of America

10 9 8 7 6 5 4 3 2 1

The purpose of this book is educational and it does not give medical advice.

This book is dedicated to the

Life Force of the Universe

and to all the researchers who

created the foundation for this book.

Contents

Chronic Fatigue and the Great Cycle of Life

1. The Nature of Threat and Defense

Imagine you are a chipmunk gnawing on a nut; suddenly, a dark shadow looms overhead. You arouse, freeze, and try to figure out how close the threat is and the location of a good exit spot.[1,2] Now you hear wings flapping and the shadow morphs into talons approaching your head. You flee.[3] Let's look at this scenario again. The first element to look at is the setting. It is outside the nest and outside the body; that is, the setting is the exterior world. It is likely warm and provides food. So in addition to offering the possibility of reward, it is also seasonal. Yet, this world presents unique threats like predation, radiation, infection, and the specific risks associated with being part of a social group. Many creatures seem undaunted by such circumstances possibly because they have and are prepared to deploy defense responses that aid survival in this particular external environment. At the same time, they are trying to complete the all-important tasks of finding food and eating. Due to the risks involved, the same creatures must be capable of sensing danger and reacting quickly, so this period of foraging outside the nest is also a period of high alertness and locomotor activity. The autonomic nervous system, which is sensitive to signs of danger, is in high gear. Not only that but it responds swiftly and unconsciously. When danger looms, we become vigilant, tense, defensive and that nut loses its luster. Being outside and in high activity mode means that this is the time period when creatures are most likely to build a nest, find a mate, and serve as lookout for the pack. A chipmunk's life distils into three main categories of tasks. The first: activity to secure resources; the second: resource conversion such as feeding, digestion, and storage. The third task is growth or repair since healthy growth proceeds once repair, if needed, completes. All tasks engage within the context of continuous self-protection or defense. Another part of this scenario is the nature of the threat. Here it is sudden, serious, and brief. Translated to human terms, it could be described as acute and life-threatening danger.

Let's say the scenario above occurs in late spring. At this point, the chipmunk is fairly lean and agile with razor-sharp reflexes - by human standards, healthy. Later, as winter approaches, the same chipmunk has gained weight, requires more energy to move, has been exposed to radiation, and may have contracted a few infections. What was originally an acute episode of danger earlier in the season, has now become a repeated event since being outside increases the odds of being hunted. In other words, the external threat has become chronic. In addition, threats from inside the body begin to manifest themselves. These include extra weight and pathogens. Not to worry, however, because the chipmunk has found enough food to allow retreat for a while. And the timing could not be better because nature's food supply is about to dwindle anyway and the weather about to be less welcoming.

The chipmunk heads to its nest and prepares it for what appears next, a sleep-like posture. Nests are usually spaces separate from and safer than the external world.

Scouring for food, feeding and storing are no longer the key goals of chipmunk life. Now is a time for repair and it can last a long time. In this state, creatures protect themselves by retreating to safe, low-stimulation spaces. In effect, they remove their entire bodies from environmental exposure and social circulation.

Hibernation conjures the image of large bears slumbering through long, cold winters. Researchers such as Kelly Drew, Hannah Carey and their teams,[4-5] however, discovered that hibernating animals are in a state of torpor, as opposed to deep sleep or unconsciousness. Although torporous creatures are motionless and appear asleep, they maintain just enough consciousness to respond to threat if they have to; they remain vigilant.[4-6] When torpor lasts longer than a few hours and extends across days, it is then considered hibernation.[6] We know now that creatures take breaks from hibernating by waking up for short periods known as interbout arousals. During such arousal, creatures like squirrels leave the nest briefly. They move around, get food, excrete, and then return to the nest to resume hibernation.[4-6]

What seems like a phenomenon associated with arctic conditions and unique to squirrels and bears, is in reality, a physiological response that is far more common than we thought. Kathrin Dausman and team[7] were among the first researchers to discover that creatures in hot climates enter torpor too and this is called estivation. For a long time, the lemur was the closest nonhuman primate known to hibernate. Around 2010, however, researchers found that the African bush baby, another primate, also enters a state of torpor.[8] The duration of hibernation varies too. It can be brief, about 10 days between interbout arousals for ground squirrels to over seven months for bears to years for locusts.[9-11] While this phenomenon is beginning to take more diverse shapes, the common thread is that retreat into the hibernating state is a response to threat, whether internally or externally induced. Hibernation has been viewed as a method for conserving resources. Viewing it, however, as a major external defense against chronic threat-inducing situations offers a helpful lens for viewing human health. Using the example of seasonal cycle, many nonhuman creatures are more active and healthier during spring and summer. As threat becomes chronic, however, they become less active and healthy and repair dominates life. Torpor represents the short-term version of repair while hibernation is a longer repair cycle.

Hibernation is generally seen as being obligatory or facultative. For obligate hibernators, like the black bear, hibernation is a predictable annual event and once initiated, continues to completion.[12] Facultative hibernators, such as the Syrian golden hamster, enter torpor, on an "as needed" basis and exit this state when it's no longer needed.[13] Humans tend toward facultative hibernation and it appears to be organ-specific.[14] We know now that the human heart, brain, and gut show states of torpor - more on that later.

When he studied the physical correlates of emotion, Walter Cannon described the well-known fight or flight reaction as an adaptive response to situations that frighten us.[15] The autonomic nervous system activates and marshals resources for movement by increasing oxygen intake and breathing rate, blood flow to limbs, and glucose availability. Later, researchers realized that creatures often freeze first before fighting or fleeing.[1,3] Freezing can last a microsecond to an hour.[16] Although movement stalls, the body is ready for action. In their description of the defense cascade, Casia Kozlowska and team present a continuum of responses to acute danger.[3] The initial response is arousal where our sensory organs, such as eyes and ears, orient toward and begin to focus attention on the possible threat. Then if the threat is real but far enough away, we pause movement and become still to evade notice; that is, we freeze. Our breathing and heart rates drop yet our major muscles tense. If the threat approaches then some of us continue to freeze, others stay and fight and the rest will run away. In the last two scenarios, heart and breathing rates rise and the brake on muscle tension is released and it is transformed into musculoskeletal action. If fighting does not get rid of danger and the opponent overpowers, then the next defense mechanism kicks in. Known as tonic immobility, the body reduces movement enough to appear or play dead. Possums are well known to deploy this type of defense. If playing dead does not change anything then we may lose consciousness and fall into a state called collapsed immobility. Fainting in response to stress is an example of this. The final stage in this spectrum is known as quiescent immobility. If we're still alive then this is the time when we try to recover from the scary event.

Let's extend the defense cascade a bit more. In addition to considering acute danger, let's distinguish now between danger that exists outside the body (external) and that which exists inside the body (internal). The defense cascade describes a range of protective behaviors. When the threat is external then protection is in the form of whole body reactions like running or making the body look big and scary. Hedgehogs do this by making their needles stand up. Chameleons, on the other hand, change color in response to danger and skunks distract enemies by squirting a smelly substance. Even human hair stands up during fear. All these external defense signals however, originate from shifts in internal biological events.

When the threat is internal, such as getting an infection or being wounded, multiple, complex pathways activate. Similar to external defense, internal danger seems to be detected by neural cells first. Following detection, neurons then prompt many cell types into action. Although immune cells defend and fight,[17] research indicates that other cell types activate in response to threat too. Cells belonging to endocrine, cardiovascular, musculoskeletal and gastrointestinal systems respond. Just like external defense, internal defense requires a shift in biofuel production and allocation. Such changes affect all cell types. In the face of danger, therefore, whole-body behaviors change externally in concert with cellular changes inside the body. It could be said that defense operates on a continuum from external to internal change. Through this lens, arousal, freeze, fight, flight, and collapse are protective behaviors triggered first by neural action. And the same neural actions prompt cascades of internal defense too. Whether these cascades resemble the freeze to collapse pattern has yet to be discerned. Threat, therefore, both activates and impacts the spectrum of defense responses from the level of the cell to tissue to organ to organism.

The defense cascade shows the sequence of behaviors used for defense following acute threat. What would the defense cascade look like under conditions of ongoing, sometimes unpredictable and inescapable stress? Stress that persists over several hours daily to months is described as being chronic.[18] Researchers such as Thomas Holmes, Richard Rahe,[19] Martin Picard and Bruce Mc Ewen[20] say that the more stressful events we experience during our lifetimes the greater the load on us. In other words, stressful events build up over our lives and have a cumulative negative effect. Challenging life events such as starting a new job, moving, or divorce all contribute to lifetime stress load that eventually diminishes our ability to respond effectively to stress. Not only do our behavioral responses become less effective, so do our biological responses. Over this time chronic stress exerts continuous cellular damage too and initially, this can be difficult to detect.

Work by Firdaus Dhabar,[21] however, indicates that negative effects of cumulative stress reduce if we can return to a low stress state before the next stressful event occurs. We can handle stressful events better if we have the time and resources to repair and rest ourselves between successive stressful situations. When this is not possible, the body continues to behave in a defensive manner. Internally, for instance, a hormone called cortisol is secreted and a neurotransmitter called noradrenaline is released. Externally, we may display anger and irritation. A vigilant state, both internal and external, predominates functioning and sustains itself as long as we experience threat. Dhabhar's work implies that the only way to mitigate sustained vigilance and the altered moods that accompany it, is to mend the damage caused by such distress. Even chronic stress, therefore, can be mitigated given adequate healing.

Although the experience of fear is unpleasant, it goads us into defensive or offensive action that increases survival odds. Certainly fear is positive for the chipmunk that survives, after feeling fear and engaging defenses. At what point, however, do our fear responses decrease survival odds? Or, is fear good or bad for us? It depends. Hans Selye wondered about this too. In the 1930s, Selye presented the idea that what we experience as fear is really a stress on our biological systems[22] and he recognized that it can have both positive and negative effects.[23] When our response to stress helps us, then it is called eustress and we experience beneficial growth. When, on the other hand, our response harms us then the stress is named distress. In their work, Picard and McEwen[20] refine this difference further into three types of stress: good, tolerable and toxic. Good stress is wanted, for instance, when we want to learn a new skill. In addition, we control it by initiating or ending it when we wish. Tolerable stress is unwanted but we have enough resources to address this type of stress. An example of this is relocation of a good friend but at the same time having enough social support to get through this event. Toxic stress is unwanted and we don't have enough resources to address it. For many, cancer is a toxic stress.

In sum, how we perceive and respond to threat is nuanced and has at least four elements. The first is a control element, do we want it or is it unwanted? The second is a resource element. Can we access enough time, help, or other resource to address the threat adequately? The third is a temporal element. Is it acute or chronic? The fourth is an impact element. How does it affect us from the cellular to whole body level? Impact depends also on threat intensity, proximity, and on our own individual defense responses.[24] The last being influenced by personal learning histories, current life circumstances, and our genetic makeup and epigenetic signature. Our learning histories tell us what works and what doesn't. Our current life circumstances indicate our state of preparation and ability to follow through. Genetic predisposition may boil down to a propensity to exert a lot of energy and fight or to exert less energy and somehow live with the threat. Here, most of our conversation centers around chronic, toxic stress, over which we have limited control and generally impacts us negatively. For simplicity, the word distress is used.

Our response to threat begins with a state of arousal, then freeze and very quickly develops into aggression or escape. If fighting or escape are impossible then we might play dead and if this does not change anything then we may lose consciousness and collapse.[3] From this perspective, one too many defense episodes may signal the need for both the organism as a whole body and internal cellular systems to change and lay low for a long time and enter torpor that might extend to hibernation. That is, an increased incidence of threat and subsequent defense responses nudge the body into hiding and a state of prolonged inactivity and extended repair.

Recall two important points above. The first is that repair or growth is one of three types of life task. The second point is that torpor is a response to threat. Link these two points and the conclusion is that torpor engages when repair demands it. Torpor is likely a response to acute threat and hibernation is likely activated in response to chronic threat. Both are periods during which repair occurs. Since both show cyclical features then internal defense activates a cyclical response to threat. In turn, this observation indicates that health has cyclical elements and research has been confirming this. Understanding human health, therefore, requires an understanding of important ideas such as biorhythms, environmental rhythms, dominant life tasks, torpor and hibernation, and the nature of our biological response to distress. In the rest of this book, we explore these topics.

2. Biorhythms

In our world, time serves a special function; it marks the rhythm of our lives from split-second to decade. We respond to two types of time signals: those inside us, directed by biological operations, and those outside us, directed by environmental stimuli such as light and temperature. Together, signals generated internally are biorhythms. We engage many biorhythms from the relatively short duration cell cycle, or cellular growth, to the monthly menstrual cycle. The circadian, however, is probably our most salient and important biorhythm. It marks human activity - from low to high - over an approximately 24 hour period of time and expresses itself through waves of biological action.

All body systems operate according to repetitive rhythms that swing from low to high activity during a specific period or length of time. Consider the skeletal muscles that move our limbs: activity is usually higher during daylight and lower at night. Cortisol, which stabilizes glucose levels, peaks in the morning and reaches its lowest point about twelve hours later, during early evening. Melatonin, on the other hand, peaks during the night and troughs during the day. When we are healthy, cortisol and insulin levels rise early and decline across the day. This rhythm aligns generally with times when we are most active. Insulin helps cells accept glucose - a key cellular fuel. In this way, the body prepares for action.[1,2] Immune cells also show circadian rhythms.[3] Levels of circulating innate and adaptive immune cells generally decline during sleep.[4] Circadian rhythms are evident too in organs such as the heart[5] and brain.[6] Beyond daily and monthly rhythms, humans operate according to seasonal rhythms[7,8] and in some mammals this shows up as hibernation.

Signals from the external environment are influenced by the motion of the earth within the solar system.[9] It takes the earth about 24 hours to orbit the sun and this is known as the diurnal or daily cycle. During this orbit the duration and intensity of sunlight and temperature change. There are also daily variations in surrounding sound, smell, movement, gas levels (e.g., carbon dioxide), and pressure. We know that changes in environmental stimuli influence human behavior and health.[10,11] Important human events like birth, disease, and death show circadian and circannual rhythms that correspond to diurnal and seasonal rhythms, respectively. Death due to coronary heart disease, for example, peaks during winter and troughs during summer. This pattern show up in both the northern and southern hemispheres.[12]

Our internal biological rhythms don't always align with environmental rhythms. This condition, called chronodisruption, can signal illness.[13] As individuals, we differ in the times we go to bed and wake up, with night owls marking one end of the spectrum and morning larks the other.[14] Such variation is not problematic until it becomes extreme. Extremes that cause chronodisruption include working night shifts or living in challenging environments like the Arctic, or at high altitudes. Misalignment between our biorhythms and earth rhythms occurs also when we age. The common denominator here is distress. When our bodies have difficulty resolving distressful events, we may over time experience disconnect from external, diurnal rhythms[15] and such misalignment can worsen subsequent responses to threatening situations whether they begin inside or outside the body. Overall when healthy, however, our circadian rhythms tend to synchronize with the diurnal cycle of night and day.

What makes synchrony between our internal biological worlds and the external world possible? Scientists discovered that our bodies have both central and local timekeepers. The central timekeeper, the suprachiasmatic nucleus (SCN) resides in the hypothalamus.[16] This brain part is responsible for interpreting clues about the external environment. We collect information about this world through our sensory organs: eyes, ears, nose, mouth, and skin. This information is then relayed to the SCN and integrated there so that we can tell time of day and season. If you close your eyes right now, for instance, you could probably tell the approximate time of day just from the amount of noise generated by road traffic and the nature of circulating food odors.

Due to the work of researchers such as Jeffrey Hall, Michael Rosbash, and Michael Young who won the Nobel prize in medicine for their discovery, we know too that organs outside the brain and central nervous system have their own local timekeepers known as peripheral clocks.[17,18] As the master clock, the SCN coordinates clocks across the peripheral and central nervous systems. In effect, the SCN operates as a conductor that orchestrates the collective rhythms of bodily systems so they link to events outside the body such as time of day or season. Specifically, our biological clocks connect our individual selves with the world outside our bodies. The result of this connection is entrainment,[19] which means that the internal operations of the body align with and operate according to environmental signals in a relatively predictable cycle of events. Our clocks, therefore, allow coordination of internal biological events, entrainment with external events, and anticipation of both internal and external activities.

In the northern hemisphere during the summer month of June, daylight lasts about 12 hours and the outdoor temperature is warm. The result is that inhabitants are more likely to stay awake longer, engage in outdoor activity and prefer to ingest cool refreshing fare like salad and lemonade. This rhythm shifts during autumn and winter when temperatures drop and the length and intensity of daylight drops too. Then, we may linger in bed longer or go to bed earlier, desire hot chocolate and stews, and be less likely to engage in outdoor activity. Our homes, communities and cities operate according to daily, weekly, monthly and seasonal rhythms. This allows us to complete tasks of daily living, such as eating, work, and rest, together. In sum, the SCN helps us connect to at least two external conditions: the physical, such as temperature and light, and the social, such as meal and work or activity times. Although humans living in a specific community behave in a fairly coordinated way across the diurnal, as noted earlier, individual humans within the same community may have circadian rhythms that differ somewhat from the diurnal cycle followed by the community as a whole and this appears to be determined by fairly stable gene sequences. The presence of both night owls and morning larks likely aids community survival since owls can guard the community at night and larks can do so during morning hours.

In addition to helping us connect with the world outside our bodies, our internal timekeepers serve another important role implied above. They signal biological task initiation and completion. When you think about it, our bodies have several jobs or tasks they complete every day and night. First, we have the task of increasing movement and getting out of bed. Then, we have the task of getting and eating food. After that, we might need to absorb nutrients and then get rid of gastrointestinal waste. Generally, we complete tasks in a sequential manner so that completion of one task prompts the beginning of the next task. So for instance, when the body uses up enough melatonin and levels fall, we begin to feel sleepy and the beginning of sleep prompts melatonin production. The result of many cells doing jobs together is a cycle of coordinated task initiation and coordinated task completion. In other words, our cellular clocks allow coordination of internal biological events beginning at the cellular level, extending to tissue formed by cells, and then to the organs made from tissue. As Nicolay Milev, Sue-Goo Rhee, and Akhilesh Reddy note,[20] this kind of task separation by time is also a way to regulate the release of potentially harmful substances made by our bodies to those specific times when such substances are used. For instance, it's best to release anti-oxidants specifically when fighting pathogens so that such substances get used up at that time and don't run rampant when they are not needed. Due to such coordination, the organism as a whole being and to which all these cells, tissue, and organs belong, behaves in an integrated way. The tasks we complete every day belong to three broad groups of behaviors that vary across the following continua: activity to rest, feeding to fasting, and repair to growth. The timing and manner of engaging these tasks are our biorhythms. In a sense, our biorhythms are how we express life.

What are the characteristics of biorhythms? First a biorhythm is identified by the length of time it completes itself, known as the period. As noted above, the circadian lasts about 24 hours, the menstrual cycle is about 28 days long, and the circannual stretches across 12 months or so. When drawn as a graph, rhythms express themselves as wave-like patterns with the slowest action at the bottom or trough and the highest action at the peak. The difference between high and low action is the amplitude or height of the wave and this information alone can tell a lot about specific conditions. Waves repeat themselves and this makes them cyclical. Another key feature of biological cycles is that short cycles tend to fit or nest into longer-lasting cycles. In terms of time, for example, seconds fit into minutes; that is, sixty one-second cycles fit into one minute and then sixty minutes fit into an hour. This results in a progression of cycles that look the same but vary by amplitude and period. Such cycles are known as fractals and they go in both directions where shorter cycles fit into longer cycles and then long cycles revert back to shorter cycles. When it comes to human functioning, our biological cycles are somewhat flexible in that we can, under the right conditions, recover from rhythm disruptions. A good example of this is jet lag. Traveling across time zones can throw our circadians out of wack with usual environmental signals. The result may be poor sleep, gastrointestinal discomfort like constipation, and reduced mental alertness. We do, however, recover from such dysynchrony relatively quickly until our biological tools for doing so become harder to access and use.

Human biorhythms display other features discovered by researchers such as Junwen Guan and team. They explored this topic first with patients hospitalized following brain hemorrhage[21] and then in a later study involving patients with severe brain injury.[22] In the earlier study, they noticed that better outcomes were seen for patients whose blood pressure and heart rates expressed circadian rhythms compared to those that did not show this rhythm. In the next study, they examined blood pressure and heart rate over ten days following hospitalization and they found something amazing. The seven day rhythm exerted a stronger influence on blood pressure and heart rate than the 24 hour rhythm. In other words, when brain control over circadian rhythm was impeded by injury, the next cycle with a longer period (seven days) seemed to direct body functioning. The reason this is amazing is because in healthy people, the circadian rhythm has more influence than the seven-day. This implies that cycles with shorter durations have more direct and immediate influence than longer-period cycles. However, when shorter-period rhythms are disrupted then longer-period rhythms activate. In other words, the internally generated circadian detaches from the external diurnal. Is it possible that, under threat, SCN (master brain clock) control of bodily functions weakens on purpose with the result that time signals generated internally disengage somewhat from incoming, external time signals? Such a state, called chronodisruption,[13] is widespread among humans and shows up in poor sleep, mood swings, fatigue, and many chronic diseases.

Not only did Guan's team reveal an association between rhythm disruption and injury, they found also a possible method for measuring brain health. The extent to which circadian and diurnal cycles align, for example, may indicate level of brain health. They made another notable finding, from research on this cycle switch or "dip." They found that biological cycles seem to arrange themselves so that short-period cycles nest within long-period cycles. For cycles to nest, they have to be similar. Guan and team found the circadian, for example, nested within the longer seven-day period. That is, human biorhythms display a fractal nature. This type of arrangement allows coordination across system parts so they can all act together when needed, a key requirement for growth. When biological rhythms are disrupted, therefore, growth is disrupted. The point here is that our biorhythms are central to health and thus quality of life.[10,11] Further, biorhythms accommodate rest as well as activity, fasting as well as feeding, and repair as well as growth. Another important characteristic of human biorhythms is that they can be reset. A rhythmic reset is any intervention that affects one or more of the three parameters of living, namely food intake, activity level, and degree of biological repair. Now popular among many health advocates, intermittent fasting is known to improve several diseases.[23] The health benefits of increasing physical activity through regular exercise, for instance, is well documented.[24] Increasing melatonin levels[25] to bolster bodily protection via the immune system is known also to be an effective approach to recalibrating biorhythms associated with poor health.

Our behaviors, thoughts, emotions, and spirituality shift and rearrange themselves while we live through the short and long cycles of our lives that are so closely connected to physical events on earth. As Pema Chodron, a Buddhist teacher, notes, "The first noble truth recognizes that we also change like the weather, we ebb and flow like the tides, we wax and wane like the moon. We do that, and there's no reason to resist it. If we resist it, the reality and vitality of life become misery, a hell" (p. 40).[26]

Let's return to the circadian. How do we know that disruption between circadian and diurnal rhythms affects health? One of the first indicators of chronodisruption is disrupted sleep, which is a change in circadian functioning. Sleep problems include difficulty beginning, maintaining, and returning to sleep and, as a result, restful sleep is eluded. Disrupted sleep is a symptom that spans many diseases and seems to be an early sign of further physical and mental deterioration.[27] Conditions that include insomnia as a symptom are: depression, autism, chronic fatigue syndrome and/or myalgic encephalitis, [28,29] Parkinson's disease,[30]

Alzheimer's disease[30] and multiple sclerosis.[31] Notice that many of these conditions are neurodegenerative. In addition, we know that sleeping patterns change with age and aging is considered a correlate of physical and mental decline. Other conditions associated with sleep dissatisfaction are: sepsis, obstructive lung disease, cancer,[32] and cardiovascular conditions.[33] One of the most significant discoveries in recent medical research, and noted above, is that night shift work is a risk factor for cancer.[32,34] Some tolerate night work better than others.[35,36] For those who can't, however, risk increases for breast cancer,[37] colorectal cancer,[38] and prostate cancer.[39] In addition, the risk increases with the length of time one does night work.[40]

In related research, sleep deprivation, which is a biorhythm disrupter, is known to weaken immune response to some vaccines such as those for hepatitis and flu.[41,42] Beyond linking circadian disruption with disease, we know also that knowledge about individual circadian rhythms can be leveraged to improve treatment. Called chronomedicine, this approach synchronizes treatment with human biological rhythms,[43] or chronobiology.[44] Many studies show the beneficial effects of giving people treatment at times that capitalize on their immune system rhythms.[32] Patients with breast cancer, for example, who received chemotherapy at 5pm experienced less leukopenia (drop in fighter immune cells) than when they received it at other times.[45] Similarly, patients with rectal cancer who were given chemotherapy at night showed positive responses to treatment.[46] Symptoms of lung conditions, such as chronic obstructive lung disease (COPD) and asthma, improve when treatment occurs around bedtime for COPD[47] and around 3pm for asthma.[48] Similarly, signs of cardiovascular disease abate when treatment is taken before sleep.[49] Many scientists and clinicians agree that treatment effectiveness depends on treatment timing.

We are beginning to appreciate how human health is impacted by internal biological rhythms and their relationship to external, geophysical and social cycles. Evident too is the link between the latter and key life tasks like moving, eating, and sleeping. The implications of these for humans are mentioned above and explored more in later chapters. Next, however, we will examine the most fundamental biorhythm of all, the cell cycle.

3. Life Tasks

Perhaps one of the most important biological rhythms fundamental to life is the cell growth cycle. It proceeds through three subcycles that can be viewed as tasks. At its most basic, there are two types of growth. One is duplicative where the same cell type multiplies, known also as mitotic or asexual reproduction. The other type of growth creates a brand new cell by splitting and combining two different entities such as an egg and sperm. This process of joining germ cells is called meiotic or sexual reproduction. Many human cells, however are somatic and grow by mitosis and this is the growth cycle discussed below.

Cells with a nucleus grow by dividing. The nucleus contains DNA, the instructions for building cellular material. Growth passes DNA to new cells. When conditions are right, one cell becomes two, then these two become four, then four cells become eight and so on until a cluster of similar cells forms tissue and the growth cycle ends. Through the lens of task, the cell growth cycle proceeds through three tasks. The first is resource gathering. The second is conversion of these resources and their arrangement to prepare for growth. Together these two tasks are known as interphase. The end of interphase is marked by a pause where conditions are assessed. DNA quality and cell health are gauged to prepare for division. If these are adequate then the cell divides (mitosis). Mitosis represents the third task, which is growth. An interesting observation here is that, under the right conditions (health), growth and repair are mutually exclusive. Either one or the other happens but not both at the same time.

Some cells don't divide beyond the pre-mitotic checkpoint; these cells are noted as being in arrest. What stops growth at this stage? Excessive cellular damage is the chief culprit.[1,2] Growth, however, stops also when a cell reaches it's final form, these are called terminally differentiated cells. Such cells tend to be highly specialized. Two types of important cells are like this: Neurons, the nerve cells that transmit neural messages,[3] and cardiomyocytes, the heart muscle cells that generate power.[4,5] When cardiomyocytes are formed, for instance, they are flagged for energy generation and this becomes their main job. Because of this primary duty, cardiomyocytes survive for as long as we live so that they can make energy continuously.[6] If they had to slow down for growth then energy supplies would be disrupted frequently with terrible consequences for us. Compare cardiomyocytes to red blood cells, which lose their nuclei early and live only a few days. New cardiomyocytes are made during our lifetimes from stem cells but this is a low frequency event and is the reason why, by our 70s or so, we still have about half our original cardiomyocytes.[6,7] Regarding neurons, research indicates that they change in response to injury and this is called neural plasticity.[8] Such plasticity allows new connections between neurons, but growth of brand new neurons occurs rarely.[9,10]

The rhythm of cellular growth aligns well with metabolic task. Metabolism refers to all the chemical reactions within and outside cells that support living. The basal metabolic rate is the minimum amount of energy needed for critical functions like breathing and circulation[11] and it changes as energy needs increase. Our biological clocks and metabolism work together to coordinate internal bodily functions and adjust to shifting external conditions.[12-17]

When Benjamin Tu and team examined the yeast cell, they noticed that it's behavior changed in a predictable way over time depending on the type of task being done.[18] They called these three major tasks "metabolic phases." The first phase differed from the other two phases by changes along two parameters: metabolic rate and the nature and configuration of specific genes that were switched on, so to speak. If we want to know the predominant function of a cell at any moment in time, then we look at the types of proteins being made since proteins are the tools through which cells accomplish major jobs. Further, the specific types of protein being made depend on which genes are activated. Genes contain DNA, the instructions for building cellular material. Every life form has a DNA sequence that does not change much during it's lifespan. However, environmental conditions (internal and external) determine which genes are expressed and which are not and this is the epigenetic signature of a life form. In the case of yeast, sugar availability is an environmental factor. When sugar is available then the sugar consumption genes are activated, which tells us that the yeast cell is feeding. Epigenetic configurations tell us, therefore, a cell's key task at any moment in time and hint at the nature of stress experienced by the body to which the cell belongs.

During phase one, Tu and team saw that genes associated with gathering, transforming, and accumulating resources needed for growth were much more likely to be expressed or switched on. Regarding phase one metabolism, the cell used up a lot of oxygen due to increased respiration (energy generation that uses oxygen) and as a result, generated relatively more carbon dioxide and water. These outputs indicated increased metabolic rate. That is, metabolic rate, was relatively higher during the first phase than the other two phases.

In the second phase, the metabolic rate dropped sharply but growth genes were activated. In phase three, the longest, repair and waste removal genes, known also as autophagy genes, were switched on and the metabolic rate remained low. What Tu and team noticed was that the growth cycle of the cell almost always happened after the first phase. From this, they concluded that growth depended on metabolic phase. In other words, whether growth occurred or not depended on the type of metabolic task being completed by the cell. So if the cell was in resource gathering or repair mode, growth did not occur, which means that timing mattered. Another important observation was that each phase had its own gene signature. This means that during growth, for instance, genes responsible for making growth proteins were active whereas genes known to direct the manufacturing of repair proteins were off. Tu's team noticed also that during any single phase, about 40 to 50% of cells were involved. In a given cell cluster, cell involvement in a specific task occurs progressively or cell participation is staggered across task. Said differently, while about half of the cells grow another percentage gather resources and another percentage repair.

As Tu and team point out, other researchers had found that the growth cycles of certain bacteria[19] and mammals[20] are influenced by external geophysical cycles and internal biorhythms. That is, cells grow at particular times only. Tu and team extended these findings by showing that the particular growth times depend on cellular readiness for expansion. The task of growth is, therefore, sequential in that, under ideal conditions, it follows a preparatory phase. Further, growth and repair occur at separate times. Tu and team found also that a third phase - repair, is a big part of cellular life.[21] Prior to this, a life-cycle was viewed generally as a two-task event: active, high energy use versus inactive low-energy use. A final, significant finding was each life task demonstrated its own metabolic rate and epigenetic signature.

Each of the organ systems that make up the human body has a specific purpose. The cardiovascular system (heart and blood vessels), for instance, transports, delivers, and collects nutrients, gases (including oxygen), and waste. The pulmonary system exchanges oxygen and carbon dioxide and the gastrointestinal system screens incoming food and drink for toxins, extracts useable nutrients and eliminates waste. Specialization and coordination of organ systems allows efficient and effective functioning of the entire organism - the human body. The major organs include terminally differentiated cells and tissue, and because they have to last a long time, they need time for maintenance and repair. Furthermore, all major organs have clock genes so allocation of time for coordinated recovery is a coordinated event.[22-24] Sleep being one example of such allocated time.

Let's return to the human heart. In addition to muscle cells, the heart includes cells that store and traffic nutrients (epicardial adipose tissue) and the heart has its own special immune cells (innate) that protect it[25] and even has its own nervous system.[26] In sum, our hearts operate as power plants mainly instead of manufacturing plants (e.g., bones) or security mechanisms (e.g., lymphatic system). Because of this job, cardiomyocytes are designed to last a long time and can accomplish this with the help of other specialized cardiac tissue that make up the heart.[7,27]

What happens when cells designed for long-term survival, such as cardiomyocytes and neurons are threatened? Most other cell types that become damaged, either self-destruct or are engulfed by immune cells, called monocytes and neutrophils, and are replaced quickly. Skin and gut tissue are great examples of this where cells turn over daily. When specialized cells, like cardiomyocytes, sense trouble, which is anything that threatens their survival, they have one of two options.[7] One possibility is to reorganize themselves to recycle cellular material and then die. Mass coordinated cardiomyocyte death is a life-threatening example of this, which is why such a move is termed "catastrophic mitosis."[28] The second option available to threatened specialized cells is - to slow down, work less, and initiate repair.[25] As Tu and team's research show, time for repair is scheduled into the life cycle of living cells. Regarding a yeast colony, Tu found that the entire life cycle took about four to five hours. Let's go up to the next level of cellular organization to tissue. The life cycle of tissue is likely longer with a proportionally longer repair time. How about organs and organ systems? Their repair times are almost certainly longer and we know that severe injury requires more time than a few good nights of sleep can offer. As Guan and team found, the blood pressure and body temperature biorhythms of people with serious brain injury operated according to a seven-day cycle.[29] We know that menstruating females operate according to an approximately 28 day cycle, where four to seven days are spent repairing the ovary and womb. We know too that many creatures experience seasonal patterns of high and diminished activity, with the latter known as hibernation. The implication of these observations is that living creatures, humans included, experience life through nested biorhythms that begin at the cellular level with the cell growth cycle. The next level up is tissue with tissue repair built into the circadian cycle. When damage extends to organs or parts of organ systems then much more time is needed for repair, maybe weeks. When a specific organ needs extra repair time but other organs don't then the more damaged organ begins to operate under a different repair schedule. It chronodisrupts. Signs of this change show up in altered neurohormonal biorhythms, altered sleep patterns, and chronic fatigue. Two hallmarks of chronic disease and aging are disrupted sleep and fatigue. It is reasonable to say now that these symptoms signal the presence of organ level injury that can not be improved by circadian bouts of sleep alone. Those with organ injury, therefore, operate under different bio-schedules. Further, their external behaviors and internal responses look a lot like torpor.

The big takeaway here is that actions at the cellular, tissue, organ, and whole organism levels are linked tightly to the time it takes to complete such actions and their related cycles. The idea of time is useful insofar as it marks the completion of one task and the initiation of the next one. In addition, all the biorhythms have the same three-task purpose differing mostly by the complexity of task operation and the period of time needed to complete the task. In other words, cycles are functionally the same but differ by period and size (amplitude) and so expand in a fractal manner across a few dimensions rather than one variable, such as time, alone. In effect the cell cycle nests into the circadian which nests into the seven-day (approximately) which in turn nests into the monthly (approximately) and then the monthly nests into the circannual. The biorhythms of living creatures arrange in a type of fractal hierarchy. This operating structure means that problems unresolved at the cellular level eventually affect tissue-level functioning which then impacts organ functioning. This in turn affects the duration and intensity of the rhythms associated with each biological level. If, for example, an organ such as the heart has to make extensive repairs, it's rhythm may disconnect from the gastrointestinal tract, for instance, resulting in chronodisruption and thus the experience of poor health.

What is the link between metabolism and chronodisruption? Evidence so far suggests that clock genes are sensitive to stress and address it by changing metabolism. In other words, metabolic shifting or flexibility is influenced by clock genes and is a tool the body uses to aid cellular repair and growth. Nowhere is this shifting more dramatic than during hibernation, when metabolism slows to a state of hypometabolism. Many forms of life, from bumble bees to brown bears, hibernate. The hallmark of hibernation is reduced energy production and use,[30,31] which translates into a big drop in the overall activity of an organism. Multiple conditions, both internal and external to organisms, initiate torpor and they all share a common feature - distress.

4. Hibernation

Hibernation is a natural defense mechanism stimulated by distress, both internal and external to the body. As they enter torpor, hibernators undergo major behavioral, physiological, and biochemical changes. These changes help them survive the privations of seclusion and environmental extremes, and seem to be necessary conditions for the purpose of hibernation - to repair, prepare for growth following repair, and, for some, grow. The first noticeable behavioral change is exiting. Creatures leave the external environment, where exposure to stimuli is greatest, and go to a different space where exposure to stimuli is reduced. Once there, hibernators select a spot, usually sheltered. The site must provide cover against predation and allow creation of a stable local temperature around the body. Such adjustment is done by arranging nesting materials to make a microenvironment.[1] In addition, hibernators control local temperature by posture, such as curling up.[2] It is notable that larger hibernators, like the brown bear, who spend more time hibernating, seem to choose sites that block signals about time of day. These signs, known also as "time-givers" from the German word zeitgeber, include light intensity, environmental temperature, and atmospheric pressure and movement. It's as if such hibernators avoid zeitgebers. Why would they do this? One possibility is that they want to weaken the influence of the SCN, which if you recall, connects bodily functioning to the geophysical changes of the earth as it orbits the sun. Cut off from such stimuli, hibernators can now focus on the business of repair. So the physical characteristics of the hibernating site assist the goal of hibernation.

By this time, the second big behavioral change occurs, which is a huge reduction in overall body movement and activity. Physiological changes include reduced heart rate, breathing rate, blood flow, and altered basal body temperature.[3-4] Basal body temperature is the lowest body temperature at rest over 24 hours.[5] Sensitivity to and the ability to regulate body temperature are key to entering and exiting torpor.[6] Importantly, creatures regulate temperature unconsciously since it is done by the autonomic nervous system, Biochemical changes include metabolic reprogramming, changes in neurotransmitter and endocrine levels, and deployment of substances that neutralize free radicals or charged particles that cause damage.[7-9]

Recall that metabolism refers to all the chemical reactions within our bodies that support living. One of the key jobs of metabolism is to turn nutrients into energy, a process called respiration. So when metabolism slows so does respiration and thus energy production and use. This state, called hypometabolism,[9] together with altered basal body temperature are hallmarks of hibernation.[3,10] Not only do hibernators use less biofuel, they switch the type of biofuel used.[11] Furthermore, many biochemical reactions involved in the tasks of daily living change too. The ability to make all these changes is called metabolic flexibility or reprogramming[9,12] and hibernators excel at this. During hibernation, not only does protein production slow down, but the types of proteins made changes too.[13,14] This shows up as alterations to gene transcription and translation, steps involved in epigenetic change. As the body enters hibernation, therefore, changes occur all the way down to the nuclei where genetic reprogramming initiates.[15,16]

To sum it up, the internal shifts instigated by torpor and then hibernation reveal how the body changes in response to threat. All these changes, however, at both the external, observable level and the internal, less observable level, move the body to the brink of survival. Extended repair exerts a high cost.[17] From the human viewpoint, hibernation is extreme: a state of prolonged starvation, immobility, and physical vulnerability. What unfolds, however, is an adaptation to distress that affects the three main tasks of living: activity and resource recruitment, feeding and resource conversion, and repair or growth. Storage involves cellular expansion and although it causes an increase in body size, it is not the same as mitotic growth which involves generation of new cells. Let's examine first changes associated with resource conversion, specifically, feeding and storage.

Some hibernators, like the ground squirrel, accumulate food outside their bodies; these are the food-storing hibernators[10] and they access stores during interbout arousals. Creatures like the brown bear, however, are fat-storing hibernators. To get to maximum fat storage, they eat a lot of food before hibernation (hyperphagia) and as a result gain extra body weight. These hibernators then use fats stored internally for nutrition instead of feeding.[11] Obtaining nutrition this way is a huge change that effects many body systems. How does this happen and what are the effects of this switch on the body? Our bodies use glucose, fatty acids, and proteins for biofuel and the extent to which we use more of one than the other depends on the organ[18,19] and our energy needs,[20] which in turn depend on the type and duration of distress we experience. Distress has physical, cognitive, emotional, and spiritual elements. Generally, during acute, high energy need, glucose is more likely to be used, but when demand declines, then fatty acids are more likely to be used. This reprogramming, which causes a switch from regular to reduced metabolism, means that some hibernators rely on fatty acids for nutrition and these are readily available via adipocytes or fat storage cells. Adipocytes cluster together to form adipocyte tissue which surrounds important organs such as the heart, kidneys and reproductive organs. There are two types of adipocyte tissue: white or WAT and brown or BAT. WAT operates as fat storage sites and these are the cells that expand when we have surplus fatty acids. BAT, on the other hand, generates rapid heat through a process called thermogenesis, a critical part of exiting hibernation.[21]

Adipocyte tissue provides not only physical protection but also nutritional and biochemical protection.[22] The process by which these stored nutrients are taken up internally by organs is quite different from the one that is activated by eating food through the mouth, which involves the gastrointestinal system.[8] The gastrointestinal system begins in the mouth, continues to the stomach, then goes on to the small and large intestines, and ends with the anus where waste is expelled. Digestion involves a lot of mechanical and biochemical work by our bodies and resident microbes all along this tract. Consequently when digestion declines, so does our need for digestive enzymes and the fuel and energy required to move food through the gut, break food down, absorb the nutrients, and eliminate the waste. Further, by relying on stored versus digested nutrients, hibernators accumulate less waste because for the most part, the end products are recycled within the body.[14,23,24]

Pre-hibernation hyperphagia causes WAT to expand until it is constrained by lack of space. At this point, insulin receptors on the adipocytes change and they stop accepting insulin because the storage cells are now full.[25] This state is insulin resistance,[26] which is likely another internal cue to stop eating and retreat. When humans reach this state, the pancreas begins to make more insulin to force cell entry but the higher insulin levels also stimulate the liver to release more glucose which leads to high levels of blood glucose or hyperglycemia. Insulin helps cells take up glucose so when cells stop accepting insulin, they eventually stop accepting glucose too. This condition is diabetes. Whether hibernators advance to diabetes is debatable, yet many show higher-than expected blood glucose levels.[20,27] What is clear, however, is that most show insulin resistance, a precursor to diabetes.[28] In addition, once these creatures finish hibernation and resume activity, insulin levels normalize; researchers describe this process as reversible insulin resistance.[29] How do hibernators accomplish this? During hibernation, they stop eating, internal fat demand starts to exceed supply and so the adipocytes become smaller. In turn, the shape of insulin receptors change and eventually adipocytes begin to accept insulin again. Hibernators test the limits of their bodies and not all of them survive the risks of hibernation.[17]

The next big risk to hibernators is immobility. Because torpid creatures don't move a lot, their muscles are not used often. In addition, muscles receive less nutrients during hibernation. Despite these deficits, hibernators tend to maintain muscle fiber during torpor.[13,30,31] Mammals have two types of striated muscle tissue: skeletal and cardiac. Skeletal muscle attaches to the skeleton and because it aids movement, it is vulnerable to wasting. The question then is, how do hibernating creatures reduce the odds of muscle wasting or atrophy? Mitsunori Miyazaki's team[32] describe this phenomenon as "muscle atrophy resistance" and view it as a process whereby protein production and break-down balance continually, since muscles consist mostly of protein. Smaller mammals, such as squirrels, move during interbout arousal and this helps muscle maintenance; however, larger mammals like the black bear shift position but don't arouse. In their study, Miyazaki and colleagues found muscle waste in black bears after about 5 months of inactivity. Consistent with this, they noticed a significant increase in protein breakdown enzymes (E3 ubiquitin ligase) and activation of autophagy (cellular waste removal) genes (beclin 1, atg7) one-week after arousal. Since these results contrast with those of other studies, Miyazaki concluded that some muscle waste occurs among larger mammals but the rate of loss is relatively low due to the protective effects of lowered metabolism. From their perspective, Shannon Tessier and Kenneth Storey[33] believe that muscle plasticity is the key feature that reduces atrophy. In addition to a decline in protein production and breakdown, they describe three other biochemical processes that allow such flexibility. The first is anti-oxidant defense which helps to control the build-up of toxic lipids due to increased amounts, circulation, and respiration of lipids. The second process is a physical restructuring of muscle cells to adapt to less work in colder temperatures. With the third process, protective protein levels increase while growth-related proteins decline.

Cardiac muscles (cardiomyocytes) present a different challenge since they have to operate continuously to pump oxygen and nutrients all over the body. Further, cold blood is thicker and harder to move. In their research with squirrels, Christine Childers and colleagues examined the role of one cell receptor particularly sensitive to physical distress, the epidermal growth factor receptor or EGFR.[34] They found that hibernation is associated with activation of this receptor which controls the cell cycle. Recall that under threat, we defend or offend. When defending, we retreat and stall growth. Translated to the cell growth cycle, this means that cells remain quiescent or in the resting, non-growth phase. Childers' team discovered that torpor is controlled by biochemical interactions that reduce growth. They found also changes in innate immune functioning that lowered production of apoptosis proteins (p-BAD protein) and increased production of another immunity protein called active capase-9 protein, involved in autophagy. Cardiac myocytes, therefore, protect themselves by slowing both cellular growth and destruction, and by changing relative amounts of dominant immunity proteins. In summary, striated muscles survive prolonged immobility due to biochemical changes that impede both muscle fiber growth and breakdown. These changes happen in concert with a shift in immune system functioning too, which brings us to the next key task of living affected by hibernation, the repair to growth continuum. Changes in the ability to engage these operations during hibernation, is reflected in altered defense mechanisms.

Curiously, during the vulnerable hibernation period, immune cell activity suppresses.[35] The number of specific immune cells in tissue and circulation drops. Innate immune cells like neutrophils and macrophages decline[36] and so do lymphocytes, the warriors of the adaptive immune system. Such suppression leads to a drop in pro-inflammatory and stabilization of anti-inflammatory biochemicals.[37] On the other hand, macro protection systems deploy. Physical isolation decreases the probability of external and internal attack. Almost complete shut-down of the gastrointestinal tract is another element of this system because it reduces the odds of ingesting pathogens just as reduced breathing reduces the odds of inhaling unwanted microbes. Less feeding results in less circulating glucose but the downside is little access to fast glucose-facilitated immune cell defense. The upside is less food for unwanted fungi or other microbes that need sugars for growth. A decline in breathing reduces oxygen and thus iron supply, which likely stems bacterial growth.

Body temperature regulation comprises a powerful defense process. Hypothermia, a drop in basal temperature, exerts a protective effect because many pathogens that live in mammals, operate best at normal body temperature, which is around 36.8 degrees Celsius plus or minus about 0.5 degrees Celsius (98.2 +/- 0.9 degrees Fahrenheit). So reducing basal body temperature reduces the activity of resident and new microbes. This contrasts with the fever response where unusually high body temperatures are an attempt to get rid of invading microbes that can't tolerate high temperatures. But humans can't tolerate these temperature extremes for long either. Smooth flow and operation of all the biochemicals that make up our neural, immune, and hormonal systems operate best within the range of average body temperature.

The first objective of extended repair is to create an unwelcoming environment for pathogens so that they are eliminated or controlled. Although offensive immune cell activity suppresses, powerful anti-oxidant and anti-nitrosative mechanisms engage.[38,39] Also, waste management emerges as another key feature of this defense shift, which makes up a large part of repair operations. The first step of waste management is to prevent new waste generation. Declines in movement, feeding, and breathing assist this goal. The next step is waste removal and recycling. Individual cells do this through autophagy. Within the cell, autophagy destroys, gets rid of, and recycles damaged and unwanted biomatter from tiny cell organelles like mitochondria.[40] Fasting, whether intermittent by stockpiling hibernators or continuous by fat-storing hibernators, triggers autophagy.[41] Waste removal and recycling creates space and valuable resources for new cells. Another key reason is to get rid of biomaterial that triggers immune cell alarm and attack. Such material refers to damage-associated molecular patterns" or DAMPs. Being a key part of cellular maintenance and repair, autophagy prevents waste build-up, promotes healing and creates conditions for growth.[40]

As creatures enter torpor, blood flow slows and oxygen supply drops. When they exit torpor, blood flow increases and oxygen increases. During these transitions, therefore, oxygen supply changes dramatically and such oxygen flux can be lethal. Creatures who experience such flux risk harm from both inadequate and excessive oxygen supply.[8,42] Cells deprived of blood (ischemic) are fragile due to low oxygen and nutrients. They, therefore, damage easily when oxygenated blood returns (reperfusion) quickly in large amounts.

Further, the body must cope also with increased levels of potentially toxic by- and end-products.[38] To address such challenges, the body deploys a powerful anti-oxidation (neutralizes unstable oxygen) and anti-nitrosation (neutralizes unstable nitrogen) system. For instance, levels of gaseous chemical messengers such as hydrogen sulphide (H_2S) and nitric oxide (NO) increase.[8,38] Not only does H_2S induce torpor,[43] it protects heart,[44] kidney[43] and lung cells.[45] Nitric oxide is a powerful antioxidant, anti-nitrosative, and mild anesthetic. The common link here is the ability of these gases to neutralize free radicals, potentially toxic substances, by preventing oxidation and nitrosation.

According to Yanhong Wei, a well-functioning anti-oxidant system averts perfusion damage and this is exactly what they found among the squirrels that they studied.[46] These squirrels showed higher levels of antioxidant enzymes such as superoxide dimutase, catalase, and ascorbate during early and late torpor and upon interbout arousal. Their anti-oxidant defense systems engaged most during the vulnerable transition phases and then returned to pre-hibernation levels, confirming the bidirectional nature of these processes. Intriguingly, Wei's team identified higher levels of one anti-oxidant in particular, hydrogen peroxide, and this was evident in the heart and brain during late torpor. Hydrogen peroxide can be destructive during usual conditions but seems to be a critical protector of neurons, and thus the organs that include well-developed neuronal tissue like the brain, heart, and gut, when metabolism drops. As a result, they suggest these tissues may be more vulnerable to oxygen deprivation,[46] a point very relevant to humans and explored later.

One last note - for a select group of hibernators, those who conceive before hibernating,[47] the immunosuppressed internal environment precedes development of the zygote (fertilized egg). This adaptation accommodates existence and growth of a foreign body, the zygote, within the hibernator's womb. Further, the protection, repair, and rest that hibernation provides comes right before an important growth event: embryo growth. In some cases, therefore, hibernation sets up the conditions for the final stage of reproduction.

Hibernation research helps us understand what a body in repair mode looks like. It disengages from the external environment, reduces feeding and displays very little movement. Internally, metabolic operations and blood flow slow resulting in reduced basal body temperature and oxygen. Yet, many hibernators survive. An alternative defense mechanism activates and this aids survival. Interestingly, shifts that occur during hibernation occur also during sleep. Such parallels help us see that sleep and hibernation differ mainly by duration or period but not so much by function and operations.

5. Sleep

Many believe that we sleep to rest yet scientists are still debating the purpose of sleep. As James Krueger and team point out, sleep is a vulnerable state because we are unconscious for prolonged periods.[1] What is worth this risk? Kruger and team propose a few reasons, beyond rest, for sleep. One is that sleep strengthens important neural connections and keeps neurons healthy. Another related reason for sleep is that it is the time when the brain's innate immune cells become janitors. The glymphatic system, which is part of bodywide immunity via lymph and lymph nodes, for instance, removes waste from the spinal cord and brain while we sleep.[2,3] Thus sleep maintains nerve function.

Sleep supports immune operations.[1,4] We know now that cytokines, substances released from our immune cells, increase during the night, particularly pro-inflammatory IL-1 and tumor necrosis factor (TNF) levels. According to Luciana Besedovsky and team,[4] these cytokines help fight infection and maintain microbiome balance. In addition, sleep is the time that T cells memorize pathogens. On the flip side, sleep deprivation increases the odds of getting an infection and sleep disruption is associated with many diseases.[5] We know too that sleeps helps to alleviate anxiety[6] and diminish pain.[7] Thus, sleep aids body-wide healing particularly the central nervous system. But is this all?

In the quest to determine the function of sleep, Junyu Cao and team[8] coalesce these findings. Synthesizing data from several studies, they found that sleep allows the massive brain growth and development that occurs during the first two to three years of human life. After that, however, the nature of sleep changes and the purpose becomes one of brain maintenance and repair. In other words, infants and toddlers need sleep to grow neural tissue mostly but as we age, sleep is used mainly to keep our nervous systems healthy. So the big shift here is from a growth dominant to a repair dominant purpose. While adults can still generate new neurons, this occurs under specific and relatively uncommon conditions. Many neurons live a long time, due to being terminally differentiated, thus repair is necessary. Further, during daylight we need the ability to deploy our nervous system fully for all the tasks of daily living. The nervous system, being the initial and main interface with the world helps us to accomplish this and works almost continuously. Recent research shows that environmental exposure and activity incurs DNA damage in all cell types. Sleep is when this damage is addressed.[9]

The emerging and uniting theme among sleep researchers is that the purpose of sleep is repair and for some, growth. Hibernation serves the same purpose. Let's examine the sleep-hibernation relationship further. The idea that sleep parallels hibernation is not new.[10,11] What may be relatively new are findings that the sleep period is the repair and growth subcycle of the circadian and hibernation is the repair subcycle of the circannual. In terms of time allocation: About one-third of the circadian (eight hours or so) is dedicated to sleep and about one-third (around four months) of the circannual is dedicated to hibernation. Since the circadian and the circannual differ mainly by the length of time it takes to complete one period, it could be said that sleep is a smaller fractal of hibernation.

Although most life forms sleep, we differ in the amount of sleep each of us needs, how we sleep, and when we sleep. Three general reasons account for such variation. The first is due to each person's unique circadian rhythm.[12-14] The second is related to sleep debt[12] and the third is the interaction of the first two with each person's individual health profile.[16] The gap between the sleep we get and the amount we need is called sleep debt and this accumulates the longer we're awake and increases pressure to sleep.[17] It depends also on how well we slept previous nights so prior poor sleep increases sleep pressure. Often, but not always, this state alleviates when we get a chance to sleep longer and compensate for sleep deficit.[18] In this scenario, sleep helps to replenish energy reserves following prolonged alertness and exertion. Regarding hibernation, it follows the active season of foraging, gathering, and storing foods and evading attack so pressure to retreat builds over the season. In addition, creatures begin hibernation at various times; there isn't a single, mass coordinated move toward hibernation; rather, there's a window of time during which hibernators retreat.[19] Creatures differ too in how long they hibernate and when they exit it. Just as our circadian rhythms are unique to each of us, so too are other biorhythms like the circannual.

Regarding health profile, Giles Vanderwalle and team[16] present the idea of individual vulnerability to sleep deprivation. Using brain images, Vanderwalle and team show that sleep disruption affects each of us differently and this depends on how we express a particular clock gene known as the PER3. The amount of chronodisruption each of us can tolerate is governed by energy expended, our circadian cycle, and the interaction of these factors with our own unique health profile. PER3 expression, being a stable DNA sequence, remains unchanged and is unique to each of us. This explains individual variation in sleep, repair and growth needs, and the relationship each of us experiences between our health and sleep.[20]

Parallels between hibernation and sleep exist in other ways: overt behavior, physiology, brain activity, and biochemistry. Regarding overt behavior, sleepiness prompts us to move away from stimulating, social environments to calmer, quieter surroundings generally away from others. The site for sleep, our beds, provide enough room to lie down and contain materials to aid physical comfort and stabilize the temperature immediately around our bodies. This type of retreat could be viewed as defensive since it's away from solar radiation, climate extremes, and social engagement. Similar to hibernation, we stop eating and reduce movement during sleep. In terms of physiology, metabolism declines[10] and body temperature drops too.[10,21] Our breathing and blood flow rates decline. These in turn cause a reduction in circulating oxygen and nutrients. Such changes are reflected in lower heart rate and blood pressure.[22] Similar changes occur during torpor in a cycling manner explained previously.

Both sleep and hibernation share similarities across brain wave patterns and stage-like nature. When Thomas Kilduff and team explored this idea, they found that hibernating creatures respond to external stimuli during hibernation and display nonrapid eye movement (NREM).[23] The latter suggests a sleep-like state and the former indicates vigilance. Regarding humans, Pierre-Herve Luppi and Patrice Fort[24] argue that we show three states of vigilance: awake, NREM activity and rapid eye movement (REM) activity and we cycle through these states daily. The implication being that we too maintain vigilance during sleep albeit low. During sleep, the autonomic nervous system remains active or "on" so that, generally, we can still detect and respond to danger while sleeping; though, as noted previously, each of us differs in the extent to which we remain vigilant during sleep. What we do share, however, is a rapid transition from the sleep to wake state once alerted. The evidence for nervous system activity during sleep comes from electroencephalograms (EEG) that show brainwave patterns during nonhuman primate sleep[25] and humans.[26] These patterns are made from electron flow (electricity) through neurons and the speed of electrical current varies depending on the stage of sleep we're in. When we're alert, faster beta, gamma, and alpha waves dominate but during sleep we alternate between alpha, and the slower delta, and theta waves.[27]

As humans transition from wakefulness to sleepiness, the sleep subcycle begins. This subcycle is made up of four to five phases where each phase starts with NREM and ends with REM sleep.[28] NREM sleep features neither dreams nor much eye movement. Brain waves move from a state of relaxed wakefulness (alpha) to deep relaxation (theta) to deep sleep (delta). The last being the slow wave part of NREM. Entering NREM requires a drop in body temperature,[21] preceded by reduced energy use (metabolism).

Alternating about every 90 minutes or so with NREM is REM sleep. Although our eyes are closed, REM is characterized by eye movement and brain activity similar to wakefulness. While muscles move little (atonia), REM still uses as much energy as the awake brain and is the time when dreams occur.[26] A similar order of events occur during torpor. Before torpor, creatures show NREM and then transition into torpor where brain activity becomes lowest. At the beginning of the interbout arousal, creatures show NREM again. Some show REM right after this and then wake up.[25,29] When humans transition between NREM and REM, brain activity (consciousness) increases briefly, a pattern like interbout arousal. Contrasting with NREM, metabolism, blood flow, breathing rate, and body temperature increase during REM. Both hibernators and sleepers show these physiological changes.

Another important similarity between sleep and hibernation concerns the order in which the transition to either sleep or torpor occurs. After reviewing several human EEG studies, Michele Ferrara and Luigi DeGennaro[30] conclude that sleep does not happen all at once across the brain. Instead it begins in the frontal areas, where most thinking occurs, and then across other brain areas until the final part to sleep is the hypothalamus. Waking follows the same sequential pattern but in the opposite direction; it begins in the hypothalamus and the frontal areas wake up last. The same process is observed in creatures as they enter and exit torpor.[31] An orderly sequence of local sleep and wakefulness occurs. Ferrara and DeGennaro draw two important conclusions from these findings. One, that the thinking parts of the brain may need the most sleep since these parts are also the most active during wakefulness. This corresponds with the concept that sleep serves a neuronal maintenance function. Two, that sleep and wakefulness can happen in different brain regions at the same time. This conclusion supports the observation that we remain vigilant during sleep.[32] Further, it may explain the experience of shallow sleep where sleep occurs but to the sleeper the experience is similar to being somewhat awake or barely conscious.

Finally, let's examine biochemical parallels between sleep and torpor. Adenosine influences both sleep[33,34] and torpor.[35] Relatively high levels of it prompt both states. Adenosine plays a key role in both cellular energy and cellular defense. Regarding energy, it is an energy building block. When three phosphate groups attach to adenosine, a high energy packet known as adenosine triphosphate (ATP) is made. As a phosphate group detaches, energy is released. By day's end, ATP loses all phosphate groups and becomes adenosine. Daytime build-up of adenosine levels parallels build-up of sleep pressure[34,36,37] and represents depleted ATP. The higher the adenosine levels, the longer NREM sleep.[36,38,39] As sleep progresses, adenosine levels decline.[40] Adenosine slows cellular activity[41] and this radiates out to the entire body. It is, in effect, a whole body relaxant. It impacts, for example, the cardiovascular system by expanding cardiac blood vessels via nitric oxide. This, in turn, slows heart rate.[42] For this reason, clinicians use adenosine to treat fast heart rate or tachycardia.

Regarding cellular defense, clues about the role of adenosine and ATP in immunity became evident in hibernation research.[43,44] Since then, extracellular ATP is viewed as a danger signal[45] and pro-inflammatory substance. Cellular stress triggers ATP release and this in turn stimulates the release of inflammasomes from monocytes (innate immune cells), which promote inflammation. Specific inflammasomes include IL-1beta, which promotes fever and IL-18, which activates T cells or lymphocytes.[46] However, when ATP is broken down to become adenosine [via cd93 and cd73], it becomes anti-inflammatory.[47] Adenosine, therefore, is immunosuppressive. At the same time, however, adenosine activates alternative defense mechanisms. Noted above, it stimulates release of nitric oxide,[48] an anti-oxidant and anti-microbial. It protects neurons by increasing brain blood flow and tamping down neuron activity.[40] Finally, adenosine induces hypothermia,[44,49] which helps to protect the distressed body.

Gamma-aminobutyric acid (GABA) works with adenosine to induce sleep[24] and torpor.[50] GABA and its counterpart, glutamate, are the most abundant neurotransmitters in the body.[51] Glutamate excites nerves and GABA calms them down. GABA levels rise during regular sleep and glutamate declines.[52] Some drugs prescribed for insomnia increase GABA levels, which assist both sleep onset and duration. Kayla Rohr and team[53] found that GABA activity changes not only daily but across season too. During days with shorter light duration, GABA peaks around midnight. When light duration increases, GABA troughs and peaks later.

As the main neurotransmitter of the SCN,[53] GABA aids coordination across organ clocks.[54] Altered GABA levels have been found among some conditions such as major depression,[55] seasonal affective disorder,[56] and Alzheimer's disease.[57] In their work on thermoregulation, Shaun Morrison and Kazuhiro Nakamura,[58] indicate that GABA operates also in warmth sensitive neurons located in the preoptic area of the hypothalamus next to the SCN. They conclude that GABA prevents engagement of neural responses and thus whole body behaviors that defend against cold temperatures. Examples include narrowing of skin blood vessels, skin hair erection (piloerection), and shivering. Recall, that entry to both sleep and torpor require a drop in body temperature. Without this decline, NREM can not commence. GABA, therefore, exerts its effects during sleep and torpor by inhibiting neural activity, particularly the sympathetic nervous system, and allowing body temperature to drop.[59] This finding helps to explain also why sleep and torpor preparation almost always involve finding or creating a microenvironment around the body to stabilize temperature there.

One of the most well-known sleep hormones is melatonin. It's release from the pineal gland in the brain is directed by the SCN in response to darkness and levels peak during the night among healthy humans.[60] In addition to having a circadian rhythm, melatonin shows seasonal changes too in humans[61] and other creatures.[62] Hibernating creatures release relatively more melatonin during the hibernating period than the active summer period.[62] While this coincides with longer darker periods during winter, the likely purpose is to support the anti-oxidant (and anti-nitrosative) dominance of immunity during hibernation. Due to this role, Dun-Xian Tan and team[62] consider melatonin a powerful protector against oxidative stress. They note two other characteristics of melatonin that support the concept of biorhythmic task shifts, a key premise here. The task to which this point pertains is the repair-growth task. They note that melatonin is made in mitochondria during darkness. At the same time the body lowers biofuel use.[63] This frees up the mitochondria to make melatonin at night since during the day one of their chief roles is energy sensing and balance. In effect, a mitochondrial task shift occurs during darkness that aligns with a repair role versus an energy regulation role. The other related characteristic of melatonin mentioned by Tan and team is that its anti-oxidant abilities help to protect hibernating brains from reperfusion injury. Since brain blood flow declines during sleep then less oxygen circulates there too. Because melatonin levels are higher, however, the sleeping brain counters possible negative effects of lower oxygen levels. Brain-generated melatonin, therefore, protects and repairs neural tissue.

Sleep is central to health and wellbeing.[3,4,18] Poor sleep accompanies many neurodegenerative conditions such as dementia[64] and multiple sclerosis.[65] Further it shows up in diseases due to organ damage such as cardiovascular disease[66] and cancer,[67] liver[68] and kidney dysfunction.[69] Aging is synonymous with declining sleep quality and some view aging as a type of disease.[70] Chronic sleep disruption, therefore, signals chronic distress. The source of this distress may come from the external environment, such as wounds sustained in a car accident, or the internal environment, such as pathogenic infection. Sleep disturbance may indicate organ shift into a repair period longer than that provided by sleep. Given the similarities between sleep and hibernation, it is likely that chronodisrupted organs shift into a hibernatory state of extended repair.

6. Internal Distress

If a fungus can drive an ant to suicide,[1] then can it do the same to us? Until discovery of the human microbiome, interest in the microbial world with regard to human health was limited largely to external intruders such as mycobacterium tuberculosis, the bacterium that causes tuberculosis or TB. Knowledge of the microbiome led to the realization that not only does this minute world compose much of what we are, it impacts our health too.[2] While the microbiome refers generally to all the microbes inside our bodies such as those that line the gastrointestinal tract, the holobiome consists of all microbes that exist on us, internal and external, including those on the skin.[3] In good health, our holobiomes protect us continuously and work for us according to a three-task framework. The holobiome helps to gather resources from both the external and internal environments, convert resources into useable biomaterial, and assist in repair or growth.[4-6] Further, the holobiome operates in biorhythms and responds to zeitgebers like sunlight and temperature.[7,8] The focus of this chapter, however, is on microbes that make us sick and trigger prolonged repair subcycles which show up as chronic internal distress among humans. Some of these microbes are part of our holobiomes already, but endanger us and become pathogenic when they grow too much or when they move to a body part that is not their usual home. Other pathogens may arrive from the external world and cause havoc with the microbiome and the immune cells that interact with it. Here we look at an example pathogen, group A streptococcus (GAS), that triggers prolonged internal defense and nudges specific organs or the entire body into hibernatory episodes. To achieve this, GAS must somehow evade immune attack and alter immune cell functioning.

Ruslan Medzhitov and team propose that three elements make up internal defense: avoid, resist, tolerate.[9] Two of these elements parallel the model of external defense where resist is fight; avoid is flee and retreat. Tolerance, however, is the new element and Medzhitov describes it as "a stress response that can help an organism endure an infection." [9] But before tolerance develops, resistant defense deploys. When the body experiences internal trauma due to a viral infection, for example, immune cells activate. The first responders belong to the innate immune system of the damaged tissue. In this case, let's say the throat is damaged. Local throat immune cells, called macrophages, act first. They then recruit local neutrophils, other fighter immune cells.[10] During the initial acute phase of trauma, these and other innate immune cells marshal an inflammatory response to destroy the biohazard. They release toxins to kill pathogens and they engulf or phagocytize pathogens. Within a few days, body-wide adaptive immune cells join the fight. By this time, the innate immune cells have sampled or marked the infectious microbe so that the adaptive T and B immune cells can recognize the unwanted hazards. The T cells attack and the B cells memorize the offending material. Such memorization trains the immune system to strengthen future responses to similar threats.[11] But such training may not occur if initial infection is too strong.[11,12] All of this fighting action is called resistance and it causes collateral tissue damage and the misery we experience during illness. Consequently, pro-inflammatory signs of pain, swelling, redness, heat, and subpar functioning materialize during this early phase of internal defense.[13]

After a few days of intense activity, however, a more anti-inflammatory phase begins. Pro-inflammatory substances recede and are replaced by biochemicals that aid recovery. Some, known as specialized pro-resolving mediators, help alleviate the damage caused by inflammation and rebuild tissue.[14] Resistant defense, therefore, progresses through different steps that begin with inflammation and end with resolution if the immune cells succeed in removing the biohazard and repairing damaged tissue.[13,15]

The scenario above explains what happens during acute or time-limited infection. It shows how immune cells are both destroyers and builders. During initial defense, they are pro-inflammatory and destructive. Later though, they become anti-inflammatory and constructive to allow repair and restoration.[16] Most of the time, many of us don't have active infections. During health we live in a state of holobiome-immune cell balance where immune cells maintain balance between destruction (resistance) and repair (tolerance). This balance reflects in fit immune cells that are ready to fight during high activity times, which means that during health we have the ability to engage resistance when needed. In effect, immune cell responses are biased toward a resistant stance during health and high activity. During repair, however, immune cell responses are biased toward tolerance and a state of immuno-suppression.

Although tolerance gives damaged cells materials and time to heal, it also makes the organism vulnerable. The organism is less able to mount an attack against any new infection that invades or grows during tolerance.[12,17] Pathogens that survive an initial host attack, hide and reduce activity (quiescence) to evade immune cell detection. When this happens, the persistent pathogen can cause more serious symptoms upon re-infection. Some humans, therefore, who survive an infection and think the battle is over are surprised by another bout of sickness a few weeks or even months later. Even childhood infection can persist into adulthood.

Imagine the shock of seeing your child change suddenly from being relatively content to being irritable, anxious, and depressed, engaging compulsive rituals, showing outbursts of unusual physical movement, and having trouble sleeping. GAS causes all these neuropsychological changes. The resulting condition called pediatric acute-onset neuropsychiatric syndrome or PANS shows up among youth and is almost always preceded by infection a few days to weeks earlier.[18] Although many recover, some endure lifelong symptoms. At the other end of the age spectrum are adults who experience bouts of neuropsychological disturbance their entire lives that expresses as fatigue, pain, anxiety, and depression. In many cases, they recall repeated episodes of childhood infection that showed up as a sore throat.[19,20] For some of these adults who experienced GAS infection as youth, it is possible that GAS persisted within a body that tolerated it.

How can this happen and how does GAS persistence affect humans? Persistence occurs when the pathogen finds a way to evade immune attack and live in the human host relatively unimpeded by body defense responses. Noted above, such a state is called disease tolerance and GAS uses a few tactics to persist during tolerance. Humans are the only known hosts of GAS which lives on the skin and in the throat.[21] In these sites, it does not cause much trouble until it manages to get past the mucus layer and colonize the outer lining of the throat or epithelium.[22] Due to special biochemicals, GAS makes tiny holes in these cells that allow entry.[23] Once inside, the epithelial cell tries to get rid of GAS by engulfing it. GAS, however, survives this defense.[24] Not only can GAS enter and survive in epithelial cells, it can do the same to immune cells such as neutrophils and macrophages.[25] Now that it is hiding, GAS bides its time during the tolerant phase of internal defense and so persists.

Victory for GAS, however, very easily alters the course of a human life. Common signs of early GAS throat infection are a sore throat (pharyngitis), swollen and tender lymph nodes near the throat, and pain swallowing.[21] These symptoms begin abruptly and for many resolve within about two weeks. Antibiotics like penicillin help with this. For some, however, GAS infection does not resolve. It survives and starts to spread from the outer epithelium to the inner endothelium. This happens because the human host tolerated GAS instead of resisting it. At the same time, switching to tolerance aids host survival. But even though tolerance spares tissue, it poses vulnerability to repeat and more severe infection. In the case of GAS, acute rheumatic fever (ARF) develops about two weeks after initial infection, which tells us that GAS has successfully evaded immune response.[26] Signs of ARF include inflammation of many joints and heart tissue, sudden, involuntary movements, and a rash, which is a sign of scarlet fever associated with this stage of GAS invasion. In this scenario, GAS strengthens its foothold and can progress to rheumatic heart disease. GAS targets heart valves in particular.[26] The resulting inflammation and inadequate repair changes the shape of the valves so that blood flow changes somewhat and causes a sound called murmur. By the time

GAS progresses to rheumatic heart disease, a condition known as autoimmunity has developed.[27]

Immune cells respond to GAS infection first by resisting it and then by tolerating it. There comes a time, however, when tolerance breaks down. The special T cells that help to tamp down inflammation, known as T regs, don't function well anymore and the attacker T cells become less responsive to T regs.[28] The immune cell environment switches back to a pro-inflammatory state but this time it is worse because now T and B cells begin to attack human host cells. Such self attack is called autoimmunity and some view it as the breakdown of immune tolerance[28] because it's the point when our immune cells can't tell the difference between our own body cells and those of a pathogen. To get to this stage, GAS uses another crucial tactic; it expresses proteins similar to human proteins. Known as molecular mimicry, this tactic confuses attacker T cells. GAS, in particular, makes proteins that look a lot like some myosin proteins, which are part of muscle tissue.[26] Not knowing the difference between the GAS and human proteins, the T cells go after both. Thus autoimmunity develops and the immune response now poses danger to the human host.

For many, living with GAS infection becomes a long series of subpar health that alternates with worse health or flare-ups. Eventually flare-ups dominate in concert with GAS persistence and growth. Many types of pathogens cause this state of chronic internal distress. Notable and recent, long-COVID is a condition that follows Sar-Covid-2 infection due likely to viral persistence and immune tolerance. Recently, researchers found that Epstein-Barr virus causes multiple sclerosis.[29,30] Invasion by the fungus, candida albicans, causes intestinal problems like bloating and cramping, and aids release of toxic biochemicals to other body parts.[31,32] All these conditions, over time, exert negative neuropsychological effects.[18,33-35] Thinking and reasoning become more defensive and narrow and the ability to concentrate declines. Mood becomes more depressed with enhanced anxiety episodes. Mental fatigue increases. In a sense, the mind does not do its job properly. One part of that job is to protect us. Neuropsychological changes that make us vulnerable therefore threaten survival and we know now that pathogens cause such changes in humans.[36,37] So, if a fungus can drive an ant to suicide then yes, a pathogen can drive a human to suicide too.

When chronic threat overwhelms the immune response, two points of vulnerability expose themselves and create conditions for pathogenic persistence. The first is when destruction falters and is incomplete and the second is when restoration is unsatisfactory. When the initial immune response is not strong enough to destroy pathogens, the ensuing tolerance phase poses vulnerability since it is largely anti-inflammatory. This is the time when pathogens that survive the initial attack reduce activity to evade immune cell detection. So, an insufficient initial immune defense is the ideal setup for pathogens to establish a foothold in the host. What about the second vulnerability point? Chronic threat conditions set the body up for another unwanted outcome - incomplete and/or unsatisfactory repair. Although immune tolerance is designed to aid repair, prolonged distress may hinder restoration. Inadequately restored cells and tissue then become another target for immune resistance. Both points of vulnerability create conditions for chronic inflammation and eventually, for some, the conditions for autoimmunity. Chronic inflammation signals biohazard persistence be it a pathogenic microbe or toxic substance.[38] Biohazard persistence and inadequate repair cause chronic internal distress that manifests as a cycle of low-grade inflammation that alternates with higher-grade inflammation. In turn, this state triggers prolonged repair subcycles similar to hibernation.

7. Chronic Distress

Our bodies are designed to return to a balanced state following stress.[1] While eustress can advance functioning toward positive growth, distress can hamper positive growth.[2] In this chapter, effects of chronic distress are explored. Chronic distress persists over several hours daily to months,[3] is unwanted, and few if any resources are available to tolerate it.[4] How it impacts neural, endocrine, and immune responses are addressed here.

Neural Dysfunction

Chronic distress influences the whole body, however, the nervous system is affected first just as acute distress affects the nervous system first. This happens because both our external sensory organs, such as eyes, and our internal sensory organs, such as the heart[5] are the first to come in contact with, and register threat. Information from the sensory organs goes to our brains, which then orchestrates neurotransmitter, hormone, immune, and muscular responses. The nervous system is affected first and this is significant for at least two reasons. First, neural networks spread throughout the body so effects are far-reaching and imbalance in one part of the network generates effects in other parts of the network. Second, neurons exert powerful effects on many different types of cells including muscle, gland, blood, lymph and immune cells.[6-8]

Regarding distress, key neurotransmitters are: adrenaline, noradrenaline, and acetylcholine.[9] Adrenaline and noradrenaline carry out sympathetic functioning (fight and flight) whereas parasympathetic function (rest and digest) acts through acetylcholine. Recall that both sympathetic and parasympathetic networks, which make up the autonomic nervous system, operate automatically and so we don't generally control these networks consciously.[10,11] When the autonomic nervous system disrupts, the resulting condition is called dysautonomia and it signals imbalance between the sympathetic and parasympathetic networks, or sympathovagal imbalance.[12] This imbalance plays out in a few ways but over-activation of the sympathetic and under-activation of the parasympathetic shows up in conditions that develop following acute and chronic distress.[13,14] Examples of these include PTSD, major depression, and septic shock.

Frequent and prolonged activation of the sympathetic nervous system without adequate time to rebalance, therefore, leads to dysautonomia. While this affects many organs, the heart and blood vessels may bear the worse effects of such nervous dysfunction since they have the most adrenergic receptors, which allow adrenaline and noradrenaline into cells. Following repeated surges of these neurotransmitters, however, cells stop accepting them; they down-regulate.[15] Given the dense neural composition of the brain and gut, they too experience the negative effects of dysautonomia.[16] In addition, as Marta Cararra and team[17] note in their analysis of septic shock, the autonomic nervous system coordinates action across organs like the heart, lungs, liver, and kidneys. So a disrupted autonomic nervous system results in disrupted communication across organs which leads to chronodisruption. Dysautonomia and chronodisruption appear together in many neurological diseases.

Chronic activation of the sympathetic nervous system affects us cognitively, emotionally, and physically.[13,18] Cognitively, our brain fear parts, such as the amygdala, arouse and attention focuses on the potential threat to the extent that reasoning abilities decline. Physically, signs include sudden onset of rapid heart beat (tachycardia), startle response, insomnia, temperature dysregulation, and disrupted peripheral blood flow. Corresponding to these signs are biochemical markers of chronic distress which include altered levels of adrenaline, noradrenaline, and cortisol. Emotionally, we experience more anxiety and depression. Behaviorally, sympathovagal imbalance provokes tense, jumpy, and defensive responses. Situations benign to many, such as grocery shopping, may provoke extreme sympathetic responses among those with sympathetic disturbance. When threat is perceived, a sudden and extreme sympathetic response activates initially and in some cases this is followed by an extreme parasympathetic response such as fainting or collapse.

The quick ramp up in emotional and behavioral expression translates as extreme fear and in some cases extreme anger too. Conditions in which extreme fear manifests include obsessive-compulsive disorder, PTSD, and phobias. A classic sign of sympathovagal disturbance is the startle response noted above. This is an exaggerated reflexive response like a yell or jump to unexpected stimuli be they visual, auditory, or tactile. Known also as poor prepulse inhibition, startle is thought to occur because the brain part that detects fearful stimuli does not control or "gate" responses to such stimuli very well.[19] Although it reveals heightened sympathetic responding, it simultaneously shows that the parasympathetic response is disturbed too.

Just as sympathetic responding changes so does parasympathetic responding.[20,21] The vagus nerve, the largest autonomic nervous system nerve and key conduit for parasympathetic sensing and responding, communicates through acetylcholine. This neurotransmitter activates muscles needed for bodily activities we do unconsciously like breathing, moving blood, digesting nutrients, creating waste and sweating. Acetylcholine is taken up by its own specific receptors - muscarinic and nicotinic. These body-wide receptors also become less responsive under chronic distress and eventually down-regulate. This does not mean that we stop breathing or digesting; we just do so in a less efficient and effective manner. For the most part, our bodies are biased toward parasympathetic responding[12] since we engage energy-intensive movement like walking or running much less frequently. The heart, for instance, shows this bias since blocking parasympathetic responding causes it to beat faster. In the absence of threat, a heart biased toward relaxation likely survives longer than one biased toward excitement.

Such observations are consistent with Stephen Porges' idea that the parasympathetic system keeps the sympathetic system in check via a "vagal brake" that's engaged until we have to deploy more energy-intensive activity.[22] According to this view, sympathovagal disturbance reflects a dysfunctional vagal brake. In other words, the parasympathetic nervous system exerts less effective control over the sympathetic nervous system. The heart sends information to the medulla oblongata in the brainstem mostly through the vagus and glossopharyngneal nerves. From there, information transmits to the rest of the brain, via the nucleus of the solitary tract, which adjusts parasympathetic responses. When we need to relax, for instance, parasympathetic functioning is enhanced and this automatically tamps down the sympathetic nervous system. In other words, when we are healthy the parasympathetic nervous system generally dominates the autonomic nervous system and sympathetic responses activate on an "as needed" basis.

One of the metrics used to assess autonomic nervous system functioning is heart rate variability (HRV). This metric represents the variation in time between heart beats. Although it gives information about the cardiac autonomic nervous system in particular,[14,23] some use it to assess overall autonomic function. Low variation means that beats occur in a fairly uniform range, that is the time between beats does not change much. This lack of change indicates a certain inflexibility in heart pumping or contraction. On the other hand, when time between beats changes easily to prevailing conditions, such as noradrenaline levels, this results in more variation between beats and suggests more flexibility in response to stress. Our bodies try to maintain a stable blood pressure by constantly adjusting heart rate and contraction. When we need more energy, heart rate and contraction go up and when we need less they go down. Flexible heart rate and contraction, closely tuned to prevailing conditions, is therefore a sign of health and reflects in relatively high HRV values. Poor health shows up in relatively lower HRV values and reveals a less flexible heart.[24,25] Orthostatic intolerance, a sign of dysautonomia, is associated with lower HRV values.[26] With this condition, movement from sitting or lying to standing evokes symptoms of illness. Dizziness, blurred vision and nausea may be experienced. These symptoms occur because the body tries to adjust to the change in blood pressure that standing up requires. For most, the body adjusts quickly via the autonomic nervous system but disruption of it impedes quick adjustment. In sum, chronic distress causes sympathovagal imbalance and this is reflected in dysautonomia, relatively low HRV values, symptoms like orthostatic intolerance, and altered levels of adrenaline and noradrenaline.

Endocrine Dysfunction

In addition to the autonomic nervous system, the body uses another tool to respond to stress, called the hypothalamic-pituitary-adrenal (HPA) axis.[13,18] This circuit controls the release of cortisol, sometimes called the "stress hormone." When the body needs a quick supply of biofuel, the hypothalamus releases a hormone (corticotrophin-releasing hormone - CRH) that then stimulates the pituitary to release another hormone (adrenocorticotrophin - ACTH) which travels to the adrenal gland. This prompts the adrenal gland to secrete cortisol which prepares the body for activity by increasing energy supply. Cortisol stimulates glucose production in and release from the liver, it prepares the heart to pump more blood via noradrenaline, and directs cells to make more ATP. As a glucocorticoid or steroid, cortisol tamps down inflammation and pain perception. In the short term, these are adaptive responses which help us manage increased demand for energy and prepare us for action. Prolonged cortisol release, however, causes many problems. Immune cell activation and the ability to feel pain are key elements of self-defense which we need for wellness. So even though it's occasionally beneficial for us to dial back pain perception and immune cell responding, we need to have these mechanisms operational when we interact with the environment. Too much cortisol results also in sustained high glucose and lipid levels that precede chronic disease.[27] Over time, cells reduce acceptance of glucose and lipids which means that the blood carries higher levels of these substances eventually resulting in hyperglycemia (high blood sugar) and hyperlipidemia (high blood lipids). Both set the body up for long-term conditions such as diabetes and cardiovascular disease. Finally, cortisol stimulates release of adrenaline and noradrenaline and, as noted earlier, repeated surges of these neurotransmitters also harm tissue.[28]

Following stress, ACTH stimulates release of another hormone from the adrenal glands called aldosterone.[29] This helps the stressed body adjust to all the changes that increased biofuel and action cause. Such changes include increased heart rate, body temperature, and sweating. Aldosterone, therefore, works to stabilize blood pressure, blood volume, water and salt levels. High levels of this, however, causes problems too, a point that we will revisit.

Chronic distress impairs HPA functioning, which relies on feedback about body-wide cortisol levels to reduce the hormones that trigger cortisol release. When cortisol demand remains high, this feedback loop disrupts resulting in poor control of adrenal gland secretions. The link between ACTH, CRH, and cortisol levels weakens. Initially, this leads to excess circulating cortisol, adrenaline, and noradrenaline. Eventually, however, the adrenal glands secrete less resulting in lowered overall levels of these substances. The situation shifts from too much cortisol, adrenaline, and noradrenaline to inadequate amounts of them. Cells begin to adjust to this new extreme by switching from a down-regulation stance to an up-regulation stance. In other words, excess causes down-regulation but deficit causes up-regulation. What results, however, is increased sensitivity to adrenaline, noradrenaline and cortisol so that when even small amounts are released they have a relatively large effect - hence for example, the startle response.[30]

Further, the initial high, sustained cortisol levels change the brain parts involved in HPA communication. The fear-sensing brain part (amygdala) grows and becomes more excitable. On the other hand, the reasoning and memory formation parts of the brain (hippocampus and prefrontal cortex) show a decline in growth and excitability.[9,20,21] In their work with military veterans with PTSD, James Lynch and team, note that such changes result in a heightened sense of danger.[31] At the same time, the ability to reason declines and and the tendency to avoid the "dangerous" external world increases.

In many diseases, the circadian pattern of cortisol release changes so that much less is available on waking and throughout the day.[32] Known as blunted cortisol, this pattern is observed among those with Alzheimer's disease, major depression, cardiovascular disease, and PTSD.[13,33] Lower cortisol means lower glucose availability. This condition, in addition to less noradrenaline and adrenaline, contributes to fatigue. In humans, therefore, altered cortisol rhythms and levels are markers of chronic distress. In this state, cortisol has less power to control inflammation and pain. Thus, lower cortisol levels contribute toward a more pro-inflammatory state, more pain experience, and fatigue.

The HPA axis and autonomic nervous system work together to meet increased demand for fuel and action. Long-term disturbance of these response systems change both sensory and motor reactions to threat. Chronic distress changes the mechanisms by which we make, release, and respond to adrenaline, noradrenaline, and cortisol. In effect, too much or too little of these substances release resulting in hyper-excitable or hypo-excitable motor responses to distress. Together, all these disturbances influence immune cell functioning.

Immune Cell Dysfunction

During acute distress, healthy immune cells remove or neutralize biohazards and restore damaged tissue. Known as resolution, this state marks the end of an acute inflammatory episode and a return to health.[34,35] According to Firdaus

Dhabhar and team, humans can handle trauma as long as we have the time and resources to repair and recover fully between successive traumatic situations.[36] As Vladimir Rogovskii notes, however, immune cells don't always progress to resolution and a state of active defense continues.[37] This state shows up as continued sickness and continued high levels of pro-inflammatory substances - chronic inflammation. Rogovskii reasons that chronic inflammation is a sign that the biohazard remains and now the immune cells are in prolonged contact with the irritating biohazard. The resulting chronic resistance means that pro-inflammatory conditions continue increasing the chances of collateral tissue damage. And the more damage, the more likely immune cells are triggered to fight.[38] In addition to collateral damage, another stimulus for immune cell attack develops. While damaged tissue may be repaired, it is not always restored to its original state. Healing is incomplete and inadequate and though functional, tissue is still injured. Immune cells sense poorly repaired cells and perceive them as threatening or "damage associated molecular patterns" (DAMPS) and try to destroy or remove them.[39]

Because tissue types differ, their innate immune repair differs too and is unique to tissue type.[40] When skin cells are damaged, for example, the innate immune cells of the skin promote clotting and scabbing. When new skin forms eventually underneath the scab then restoration completes. If, however, the innate immune cells are unable to repair the skin properly then an ulcer may form and is a sign of inadequate repair. Inadequate repair of muscle tissue results in fibrosis. When neurons are not repaired fully and correctly then amyloid deposits build up. Inadequately repaired blood vessels form atherosclerotic plaque. All these repair failures contribute to a state of chronic low-grade inflammation[41] and aging.[42] Inflammatory status can be assessed by a blood test for C-reactive protein (CRP) levels. The range for low grade inflammation is 3 to 10 mg per liter.[43]

Recall that during a short-term immune defense event, immune cells shift from being destroyers to builders and this allows trauma resolution. When resolution can not be achieved during short term immune defense then a longer defense cycle begins. The cellular environment has a new element, long-term presence of a biohazard. In response to this changed environment, cells reprogram. In other words, chronic biohazard presence provokes epigenetic shift.[41,44] This shift translates into a longer defense phase which means prolonged resistance. Rogovskii argues that prolonged resistance results also in prolonged tolerance.[37] This is how immune cells adapt to the new (distressful) cellular environment. As long as the host survives and the infection does not invade and overwhelm healthy tissue, this new altered state materializes into chronic inflammation. Despite having low-grade inflammation, many are able to complete activities of daily living even though such a condition causes pain and discomfort.

Just as acute inflammation includes phases of resistance and tolerance, so does chronic inflammation, albeit on a longer time frame. We are familiar with the kinds of conditions that display chronic inflammation; they include diabetes mellitus, cardiovascular disease, and chronic fatigue syndrome. An important discovery during Covid-19 was that obesity increased the odds of dying from SARS-Cov-2 infection.[45] Obesity confers a state of low-grade inflammation.

This happens because the adipocyte tissue, where extra fatty acids are stored, can no longer accommodate the enlarged adipocytes or cells that make up this tissue and some become damaged or die off. Such a setting also activates pro-inflammatory immune cell activity and thus the cycle of chronic inflammation.

The conditions above involve phases of resistance and tolerance that operate in a cellular environment that is now forced to accommodate a pathogenic entity. Further, such accommodation takes on a more permanent stance due to epigenetic shift. For those with chronic inflammation, this translates into phases of subpar health (tolerance) that alternate with phases of extremely subpar health or sickness (resistance). Thus a new normal emerges for those with chronic disease. In the case of progressive deterioration, the resistant phases eventually outlast tolerant phases marked by increased pro-inflammatory biochemicals and the experience of more extreme illness. Further, a body that operates in a state of low-grade inflammation is more vulnerable to other threats such as new infection.

In sum, chronic distress disrupts both sympathovagal and HPA axis functioning. These disruptions disturb immune cells too which have to operate in extreme pro-and anti-inflammatory settings. Altered immune cell behavior results in chronic inflammation that displays as prolonged periods of tolerance and resistance. Under these conditions, tolerance becomes a low-grade pro-inflammatory state that alternates with resistance, a more intense pro-inflammatory state. If we can't return to a low-stress state long enough to restore properly then future responses to distress are compromised. The resulting bias toward pro-inflammatory responses amplifies vulnerability to chronic disease and other threats.

8. Chronic Distress and the Heart

Among humans, heart muscles can seize up in such a manner that the shape of the heart changes. The left ventricle balloons and because of the resulting bulbous shape, this condition is called takotsubo, the Japanese word for octopus trap.[1] Takotsubo occurs in response to a sudden, big stress and more often in postmenopausal women.[2] Since it often, but not always, follows a distressful event, it is called also broken heart syndrome. While physical trauma can trigger takotsubo, it is notable for occurring in response to psychological trauma, such as the sudden death of a partner. What happens is considered a transient acute heart failure[3] and biomarkers include increased troponin and B-type natriuretic protein, both of which signal inflammation. The resulting reduced outflow of blood causes chest pain, shortness of breath, and dizziness. Some proceed on to the fainting stage of defense.

Recall that the sympathetic nervous system activates when threat is encountered and part of this response involves the release of noradrenaline and adrenaline. With takotsubo however, the noradrenaline and adrenaline surge is so big that these neurotransmitters overwhelm heart muscles (cardiomyocytes) and cause extreme contraction or spasm.[4] Consequently, the neurotransmitter surge is considered the cause of takotsubo. Some conditions make takotsubo more likely and they are: anxiety, neurological disturbance, and Raynaud Syndrome.[5] Further, in their research, Lucy Norcliffe-Kaufman and team found that the autonomic nervous system operates differently in women who experienced takotsubo compared to women who did not.[5]

Among the healthy, sympathetic and parasympathetic responses occur within a fairly stable range. Among those who experience takotsubo, however, the immediate sympathetic response is more exaggerated than the parasympathetic response, which means that they are relatively more easily startled and have more difficulty returning to a relaxed state after being frightened. In terms of the defense cascade, takotsubo resembles a defense response that occurs in the context of sudden, acute, and inescapable threat that affects heart muscles to the extent of sometimes leading to collapsed immobility. In effect, the initial response to threat marshals an extreme sympathetic response but when this does not work then an extreme parasympathetic response occurs. Takotsubo presents as acute and temporary dysautonomia.[6] An important point here is the involvement of adrenaline and noradrenaline. Although increased levels of these neurotransmitters may explain cardiomyocyte spasm, heightened sensitivity to them is another possible explanation. It's notable that once experienced, takotsubo resolves within a month or so as long as no other complications arise and the body is given an opportunity to heal.[7] Another important point here is that takotsubo shows a direct link from distress to heart dysfunction, albeit temporary. Further, this unusual neural response has a ripple effect that provokes atypical blood vessel, cardiomyocyte, immune cell, and adrenal gland responses. Takotsubo shows us what happens to some hearts following a sudden, inescapable and big threat that is time-limited. What happens, however, when threat continues and is perceived as being inescapable? To answer this question, let's examine internal responses to chronic distress in more detail.

We know now that both short and long-term distress challenges the heart. We know that cardiomyocytes live a long time and so need continual maintenance and repair. When mending can't be achieved adequately within the circadian rhythm then the heart, and possibly other body parts, shift into a longer repair cycle. Finally, a sick heart directs the rest of the body to slow down. If you were a heart, what would you do to prevent further damage and aid repair? Probably the first directive would be to remove oneself from demanding environments such as work and social encounters. These settings require physical and psychological effort and so withdrawing from them means that the body does not have to maintain high level functioning. Further, withdrawal reduces the risk of encountering and experiencing challenging events and unpleasant emotions such as anger and anxiety, which would hamper repair. A second directive of the ailing heart would be to reduce overall physical activity or to immobilize.

An important way to do this would be to cut down available energy supply (ATP). Heart muscles have the most mitochondria in the body and so make a lot of ATP. When these cells operate at a subpar level then less energy is generated which contributes to fatigue. If the body insists on moving anyway then available ATP is used up resulting in the experience of tiredness and for some illness after physical activity, known also as post-exertional malaise. What else could the body do to discourage movement? It could make gross movement painful and unappealing. Humans with ongoing heart dysfunction tend to avoid rigorous exercise due to the fatigue and pain it causes. In sum, early signs of chronic cardiac distress are withdrawal and a big reduction in body movement. Such responses look a lot like torpor.

Takotsubo is the heart's response to acute threat - torpor. Prolonged threat appears to push the heart beyond torpor into hibernation. In the 1980s Shahbudin Rahimtoola, a cardiologist, described a patient with coronary artery disease caused by a partially blocked artery entering the left ventricle.[8] As a result of this condition, parts of the left ventricle wall did not move. After getting nitroglycerin, however, previously motionless areas began to contract again. What appeared to be dead heart muscle, was in fact nonresponsive muscle. Rahimtoola described this condition as hibernating heart. The organ thought to work continuously throughout our lives did not; sections of it affected by reduced blood flow (due to the partially blocked artery) stopped moving but the other parts continued to contract and dilate. Although the left ventricle functioned inefficiently, it remained viable, but how? According to Robert Kloner a longtime cardiovascular medicine researcher, the motionless cells survived by adapting to the stress of low blood flow and they did this by reducing metabolism and thus the amount of work those cells could undertake.[2] In the face of reduced transport operations, one of the most hard-working organs in our bodies, the heart, adapted by switching into hypometabolic mode, a key feature of hibernation. It's important to note that even though this condition is called hibernating heart, only part of the heart hibernates (i.e., sections of the left ventricular wall) not the entire organ. Since these observations, other examples of resurrected heart muscle tissue have been discovered. Two notable types are Takotsubo cardiomyopathy described above, and neurogenic stunned myocardium.[9] The latter results from damage to vessels that supply blood to neural tissue and causes conditions such as stroke or bleeding. "Sympathetic storm" is common to both conditions and this means that a big surge of noradrenaline seems to trigger both of them yet neither involve full-blown myocardial infarction, both are reversible, and both have been observed in humans.

When cells switch energy production from one that uses oxygen to one that does not (i.e., anaerobic respiration), specific end products are made. One of the most familiar is lactic acid. Evidence of lactic acidosis is a blood pH that is less than 7.34 and circulating lactic acid greater than 5 nanomoles per liter. Severe lactic acidosis is considered a medical emergency that has long been associated with heart disease. In view of such gravity, few studies have examined the effects of lactic acid on humans. However, Hanna Schotola and colleagues were able to obtain heart tissue from eight patients with end-stage failing hearts who had heart transplant surgery.[10] The scientists induced mild lactic acidosis in the less scarred tissue (right ventricle). Their results confirmed the generally accepted idea that acidosis reduces the heart's ability to contract. They found also that mild acidosis impaired the beta-adrenergic response, so the cardiomyocytes stopped responding to isoproterenol, a proxy for adrenaline and noradrenaline. Not only did mild acidosis reduce pumping ability, it slowed down all the steps involved in stimulating a heart beat from the initial electrical signal that starts the process of contraction to its completion. It is reasonable to say that end stage heart failure is a hypometabolic condition since the presence of relatively high levels of lactic acid is evidence that mitochondria have switched to the less efficient, anaerobic method of generating energy. At the same time, this indicates also that the mitochondria have shifted into extended repair mode. The takeaway here is that lactic acidosis is a biomarker of stressed mitochondria.[11] On the other hand, mild lactic acidosis may act as an adaptive mechanism. It slows heart pumping and blocks adrenaline, noradrenaline,[12] and similar biochemicals.[10] The latter control sympathetic storm. The former induces heart relaxation. Both responses, therefore, tamp down sympathetic over-activation. In addition, lactic acid can be converted by the liver to make pyruvate, a key biofuel precursor. Mild lactic acidosis also mitigates reperfusion injury[13] caused by infusing oxygen-rich blood back into the heart as part of treatment. Further, concomitant increases in nitric oxide and adenosine help protect the heart from reperfusion injury.[14] What is a concerning correlate of heart failure may be a clue to an underlying state of altered, adaptive metabolism.

A time arrives, however, when metabolic shift becomes maladaptive. A shift that continues long-term indicates loss of metabolic flexibility which in turn reduces efficient energy supply. Researchers such as Julia Ritterhoff and Rong Tian discovered that damaged heart muscle shifts from using fatty acids mostly for fuel to using glucose and ketones mostly.[15] While this switch provides ATP, it does so at a cost when energy demand increases under stressful conditions.[16] Under chronic distress, this shift becomes more permanent because the mitochondria remodel to adapt.[17] Such remodeling, however, results in reduced flexibility to use other types of fuel such as fatty acids. Sustained reliance on glucose and ketones for fuel eventually damage mitochondria. As Bo Zhou and Rong Tian[16] put it, "they become failed power plants." The failing power plant is now more vulnerable to calcium overload that causes the mitochondrial wall to break and release inner material. This material includes cytochrome C, reactive oxygen species (ROS), and mitochondrial DNA [mtDNA], all of which signal and trigger cell death. But this is not all because these biochemicals, once outside the cell, activate the innate immune response. Mitochondrial DNA, in particular, does this by prompting inflammasomes into action. Heightened inflammation and cell death (apoptosis) result in heart muscle dysfunction. This impacts the heart's ability to dilate enough for adequate filling or to contract enough for adequate blood distribution. Heart disease results from either state. Zhou and Tian[16] note that reducing energy demand by using beta-blockers, which shield heart muscle from adrenaline and noradrenaline, improves survival. Drugs that aid vasodilation, such as nitroglycerin, improve survival too.

Let me mention one other important, related observation. Humans have known for a long time that reducing metabolism by reducing body temperature is protective. This is why during heart surgery in countries such as Russia physicians use ice to cool the body down.[18] More recently, this approach has been used successfully in the west following adult cardiac arrest.[19] The point here is that lower metabolism and thus lower body temperature protects nervous tissue following heart trauma. In addition, the initial mild lactic acidosis generated during hypometabolism may impede injury and assist mending.

What do we know so far? Both acute and chronic distress affects the heart. Heart function depends on the health of long-lived cardiomyocytes that rely on continual repair and maintenance of healthy mitochondria. When these tasks can't be achieved adequately within the circadian rhythm then the heart shifts into a longer repair cycle that displays a different bioenergetic signature. A sick heart directs other parts of the body to slow down. Put another way - fatigue signals an ailing heart.

Fatigue

Consider this symptom cluster: fatigue, illness after physical activity (post-exertional malaise), peripheral pain, poor sleep and depression. A condition exists that is known for such symptoms. Until relatively recently, this condition baffled researchers, seemed to have no cure, and many who suffered with it were resigned to the fate of a disease that just worsens over time with little hope for recovery. One name for this condition is chronic fatigue syndrome (CFS) and it appears to show how a body under chronic distress might behave.[20] In addition, CFS exists in a biological environment that sets up the conditions for heart disease to develop.[21] We'll explore this relationship next with an emphasis on fatigue.

From the perspective of those with CFS, fatigue is experienced as an unremitting exhaustion that lasts all day long over days and weeks.[22] According to one official description, chronic fatigue is a kind of tiredness not helped by rest, is not caused by physical activity, and occurs often enough that the ability to work and socialize declines steeply.[23] The reason this fatigue is a problem is that it makes the activities of daily living more difficult to do; small tasks seem like big challenges that require inordinate effort to complete. Further, physical exercise or most types of physical exertion increase exhaustion and may even cause the experience of unwellness. This a particularly important point because for many, physical exercise invigorates and is considered a cornerstone of optimal health practice. Yet, it is mostly contra-indicated in chronic fatigue conditions because of limited physical capacity to do it and the unpleasant after-effects. Examples of this phenomenon are reflected in the following statements from those with CFS: "I felt exhausted all the time" (Chris Mole),[24] "It's like the flu mixed with a bad hangover, it's like walking through mud" (Sarah),[25] "At 43, my productive life may well be over" (Brian Vastag).[26]

As an early symptom of heart distress, this type of fatigue is particularly challenging because generally it is not corroborated with typical biomarkers such as elevated troponins or unusual heart rhythms. Those with CFS, therefore, are often told there is no underlying physical reason for their fatigue.[22] When commonly used methods to determine physical illness yield little information, the implication is that the fatigue is "all in the patient's head" (psychosomatic). Such messages may lead those with CFS to believe that their illness experience is invalid and can be very discouraging to those who know that something is amiss with their bodies. Further, in certain sociocultural groups, such fatigue may be interpreted as an unwillingness to participate in social and occupational duties. Reactions like these may contribute to the depression that many with CFS experience and cause some to underplay or not seek help for their symptoms. Given this, CFS may (until long-COVID) be an under-reported condition.

What could explain chronic fatigue and how is this related to heart function? We can agree that heart disease evokes concern because it predicts premature death. Probably one of the most nefarious elements of it is the apparent lack of obvious warning signs, akin to being a stealth killer, especially among post-menopausal women. Two huge clues, however, reveal themselves early and these clues are fatigue and dysautonomia. Next, we will examine possible explanations for chronic fatigue through the lens of CFS.

9. Chronic Fatigue Syndrome

One of the most elusive conditions to emerge among modern humans is CFS. Even though there are about 20 definitions of CFS globally; chronic fatigue, post-exertional malaise, unsatisfactory sleep, and cognitive problems comprise the top criteria across these definitions.[1,2] Such features of CFS, however, lethargy and blunted ability and desire to engage in both mental and physical activity, align also with depression. Another important general aspect of CFS is the long-term or chronic nature of it with recurrent periods of relief and exacerbation.[3] CFS is progressive in that it worsens over time adding to the burden of this condition. Females over 40 is the group most likely to be diagnosed with CFS but it prevails also among males and youth. Corralling the whole concept of CFS presents a challenge not only because of broad demographics associated with it, but because of the vast symptom variations across those with CFS and the lack of a sound diagnostic test.[2-4] Note that an important outcome of these key symptoms is reduced physical activity, which worsens and may even maintain CFS.

The link between torpor and CFS was observed early, if not first, by Marian Lemle.[5] When her daughter changed from being a motivated and active teen to one that had difficulty getting out of bed, Marian researched possible reasons for such a dramatic shift.[6] She discovered that relatively high levels of hydrogen sulfide (H_2S) due to poorly functioning mitochondria might be implicated with such changes. At that time, however, her discovery did not gain immediate traction. Fast forward to 2020, it turns out that H_2S is made in relatively high levels by hibernating creatures[7] and others have since agreed that altered mitochondrial activity accounts for CFS.[8,9] Marian Lemle was on the right track.

A few years later, Robert Naviaux and his team identified the metabolomic profile (levels of many different biochemicals generated during metabolism) of CFS.[10]

Compared to those without CFS, study participants with CFS showed a pattern of metabolism consistent with hypometabolism, that is, reduced metabolism. Because of this, Naviaux too likened CFS to the state of dauer, a developmental phase during which worm larva become almost lifeless.

Meanwhile in England, Sarah Myhill - a physician with CFS, began to link CFS to damaged mitochondria. She reasoned that since mitochondria made a lot of ATP, damage to them would cause fatigue.[11] Together with Norman Booth and John McLaren-Booth, they developed an ATP Profile Test to measure the amount of ATP in neutrophils (immune cells) at various stages in its manufacture and recycling. When they compared people with CFS to those without it, they found that the lower the level of ATP the worse the symptoms. Their work, and that of others, links CFS to disrupted bioenergetics. Indeed, outcomes of many studies confirm irregular energy generation patterns among those with CFS,[8,12-14] which brings us back to the common denominator of mitochondrial dysfunction.

Or, is it dysfunction? Naviaux, in a 2012 article, suggests that what looks like dysfunction might really be an adaptation to distress.[15] His view is that excessive production of reactive oxygen species (ROS) by the apparently damaged mitochrondria is a tactic to "shield" them and protect the cell. Further, earlier research by Michael Maes and Frank Twisk[16] indicate that those with CFS tend to have higher levels of ROS. Since then, higher ROS and the inflammation caused by these free radicals have been implicated in many conditions such as depression.[17-19] Moreover, in these conditions, reactive nitrogen species (RNS) are found alongside higher levels of ROS. In sum, bodies under distress appear to make relatively higher levels of substances like H_2S, ROS, and RNS compared to those without such conditions. All these substances are considered toxic.

Why would a distressed body make "toxins?" At this point in time, researchers believe that such toxins serve to mitigate even more dangerous toxins such as those made by internal pathogens (e.g. Borrelia, bacteria that cause Lymes Disease) or by exposure to environmental toxins like mercury, or even toxins made by the body as a result of ingesting foods that have the potential of becoming toxic once ingested such as 4-hydroxynonenal (4-HNE).[20] What these effects confirm, however, is that mitochrondria though known as cellular powerhouses play another important role in human health. This is their ability to make protective biochemicals such as melatonin and H_2S.[21,22]

In his book, Neil Nathan categorizes CFS together with a set of conditions such as Lyme disease and mold allergies due to their overlapping symptoms.[23] What's compelling is the relative obscurity of some these symptoms across the general population. Take for example, olfactory (smell) sensitivity, metallic taste sensation, heightened sensation of static electricity, and salt cravings - these fairly unusual effects are common across conditions that Nathan terms chronic environmental illness. Interestingly, such symptoms are reported also among those with adrenal insufficiency.[24] How are the adrenal glands implicated? Recall, they're where cortisol, adrenaline and noradrenaline are made. During chronic distress the adrenals initially release a lot of cortisol, which in turn results in release of adrenaline and noradrenaline. From prior discussion, we know that high circulating levels of these substances eventually cause the adrenal gland to reduce production of them. In effect, the adrenal glands begin to underperform. When cortisol drops so do adrenaline and noradrenaline. The relative scarcity of adrenaline in particular means that cells make it easier for the scarce adrenaline to enter. In other words, they upregulate. What results is increased sensitivity to adrenaline so that when even small amounts are released they have a relatively large effect - hence for example, the startle response.

These diverse symptoms, therefore, are linked also by what seems to be a very sensitive, reactive sympathetic nervous system response to toxins. In addition, such symptoms may be tied to inflammation caused by chronic distress that results from other types of trauma experienced over the course of a human lifetime. In addition to the adrenal glands, therefore, both nervous and immune activity figure large in CFS. Gerwyn Morris and team were among the first to recognize the link between CFS and dysautonomia.[25] Their review indicates that about 90% of patients with CFS present with dysautonomia marked by increased sympathetic responses and decreased parasympathetic and vagal nerve activity, and low HRV values.

In their research, Franziska Sotzny and team found immune cell irregularities in CFS.[4,26] They discovered that the body's own immune cells were attacking body cells, a condition called autoimmunity.[26] Although autoimmunity in CFS had been discerned earlier by other researchers.[27-29] Sotzny found that two specific types of receptors were being attacked, the adrenergic (beta2) and muscarinic (M3). Both are key to sympathetic and parasympathetic functioning since adrenergic receptors allow noradrenaline and adrenaline into cells and muscarinic receptors allow acetylcholine into cells. Destruction of such receptors by immune cells implicates both the ANS and immune response. They noted further that disruption of beta2-adrenergic and M3 muscarinic receptors, which help to dilate central blood vessels, might cause blood flow problems in the periphery. In their study, Nadja Scherbakov and team[30] confirm that those with CFS have peripheral endothelial dysfunction and the severity of it relates directly with the severity of CFS symptoms. Lower blood flow reduces oxygen (hypoxia) and nutrient supply and this state may account for some CFS symptoms. In effect, the vascular system emerges also as an important player in CFS, an idea that Kazuhiro Yoshiuchi and team suggest in 2006.[31]

By now, it is reasonable to agree that a distressed cardiovascular system causes fatigue. Heart muscle cells have the most mitochrondria of all other cells. So, mitochondrial adaptation to distress, due to elevated toxins and other factors, exerts a big affect on the heart. Toxins come from other sources too. As noted above, mitochondria make toxins as a protective mechanism. Microbes, like viruses, make toxins. Humans are exposed to all kinds of environmental toxins that make their way into the body, sometimes via food. Those with CFS have relatively higher levels of bio-toxins[32] which activate a chronic pro-inflammatory immune response and, for some, autoimmunity.

Noted above, autoimmunity is part of the CFS picture. It turns out that all kinds of autoimmunity develops in this condition.[33] One of the first types of autoimmunity noted in CFS was antiphospholipid syndrome (APLS).[28] Here, immune cells target a protein involved in blood clotting. Ordinarily, clotting is a wanted event because it slows bleeding and is part of the repair process. Too much clotting, however, means that the repair process has broken down. With APLS, blood clots more readily and can lead to thrombosis. As long as antibody levels remain low, then platelet clumping (aggregation) and thus thrombosis is less likely. APLS becomes problematic, however, when antibodies increase and cause thrombi (clots) to form. In extreme cases, APLS can progress to body-wide clotting problems. Unwanted thrombi show up in blood vessels and the heart and can block blood flow. APLS, therefore, affects the cardiovascular system significantly and associates with vessel thrombosis, valve disease, coronary artery disease and dilated cardiomyopathy.[34]

Consistent with cardiovascular involvement, APLS is a sign of stressed mitochondria.[35] Some damaged mitochondria self-destruct (apoptosis) or prompt autophagy, both consequences trigger a pro-inflammatory response.[35]

Other compromised mitochondria change their metabolic patterns and as a result generate less ATP.[36] Such a state contributes toward chronic fatigue. In their research, Olga Danilenko and team[33] confirm the presence of APLS markers in CFS, certainly those associated with mitochondrial disruption. Although they found a few different types of autoimmunity, most targeted nerves, indicating the presence of neuroinflammation and nerve damage. In addition, they found autoantibodies against the adrenal glands where cortisol, adrenaline and noradrenaline are made.

Regarding CFS, therefore, neural, hormonal, and immune responses show disturbance. Mitochondrial disruption and elevated toxins seem to explain such disturbance. Extreme immune disturbance shows up as autoimmunity and those with CFS show a few different types of autoimmunity. One meeting point of chronic internal distress in CFS appears to be the adrenergic and muscarinic receptors that exist on nerves, adrenal glands, immune cells, and blood vessels. And because these receptor types are abundant especially in the heart and vascular system then their role in the cardiovascular manifestations of CFS is significant. We will discuss this topic next.

10. Chronic Fatigue Syndrome and the Cardiovascular System

Previously, we examined the relationship between an ailing heart and chronic fatigue with a focus on mitochondrial disruption. The role of toxins and autoimmunity were explored too. Below, we talk about blood distribution and flow disturbance and how they likely affect other CFS symptoms such as Raynaud's Syndrome, orthostatic intolerance, and cognition.

Studies show that those with CFS experience reduced blood distribution to hands, feet,[1,2] and brain.[3] This happens for a few reasons, however, key ones are: blood vessel disturbance, too much sympathetic neural activity, and blood volume irregularity and physical deconditioning.[4] A layer of cells line the circulatory blood vessels which extend body wide. Known as endothelial cells, they inhabit the inside of both blood and lymphatic vessels. All capillaries, arteries, and veins share this inner lining. The endothelium contacts blood and lymph directly and so it mediates communication from the rest of the body, particularly the brain and heart, to blood and lymph. Important jobs of the endothelium are to: maintain blood distribution, stabilize blood pressure, allow substances to both reach and be removed from tissue, and assist the immune response.[5] The endothelium controls blood flow by directing the muscles and elastic fibers that surround blood vessels to narrow (constrict) and widen (dilate or relax). Vascular tone describes the extent to which a blood vessel is relaxed or constricted;[6] high tone means more constriction. The endothelium makes substances, such as nitric oxide (NO), that relaxes vessels, and substances, such as endothelin, that constricts vessels. Imbalance between relaxants and constrictors causes endothelial dysfunction (ED).[7] Imbalance results from many factors both due to blood flow dynamics and content of blood or lymph. What's relevant to CFS, however, is that endothelial function predicts heart problems[8] and is associated with many CFS symptoms.

One of the most important effects of ED is disrupted vascular blood flow and thereby distribution. Although the endothelium makes its own relaxants and constrictors, it is influenced also by relaxants and constrictors from nervous and endocrine tissue, such as adrenaline and noradrenaline. Following stress and thus increased release of adrenaline and noradrenaline, blood flow to fingers, toes and likely brain drops.[9] This occurs because the endothelium in those body parts constricts. Such narrowing aids blood flow to body parts needed for swift movement like the skeletal muscles, heart, and liver. In those with CFS, disruption of the endothelium results in excessive blood vessel constriction in the periphery, which creates the set-up for Raynaud's Syndrome, orthostatic intolerance, and cognitive problems.

Those with Raynaud's Syndrome experience sudden coldness and numbing in fingers and toes, which turn white and then blue and can stiffen.[9] Constriction of blood vessels in these body parts follows cold exposure mostly, and sometimes other types of distress, When the vessels narrow, they receive less oxygen and heat from blood and so change color and become cold. In some cases, exposure to extreme cold such as touching ice, can be painful. About one in ten experience Raynaud's and it is associated with many autoimmune conditions such as lupus or rheumatoid arthritis. The incidence among those with CFS is over 50%.[10] It is a temporary condition since episodes end once adequate blood flow returns and skin turns red. For most, tissue is not damaged. That it is experienced at all, however, indicates endothelial disturbance. Further, while Raynaud's may seem relatively benign since it is transient and reversible, a study completed by Paul Nietert,[11] found that it was associated with earlier death among older adults in general and related to cardiovascular-related death among Caucasians in particular. What we're discovering is that Raynaud's is not a condition that exists alone. Rather it is one of a cluster of ED symptoms. Another related sign is orthostatic intolerance.

Orthostatic intolerance is the sensation of sickness when body position changes, such as from sitting to standing, or when standing too long in one position. It happens also when body fluids and salts are unbalanced, a body is in hot environments, and as a response to sudden stress. The symptoms include light-headedness, dizziness, headache, nausea, blurred vision, and fainting. Orthostatic intolerance occurs because the cardiovascular system does not compensate quickly enough when there's a big shift in blood volume from one body part to another. Vasoconstriction and heart rate are inadequate to provide the needed blood flow adjustment.[12]

A few types of orthostatic intolerance exist but those with CFS experience two types. One is orthostatic hypotension where blood pressure drops within three minutes of a position shift. The other type is postural orthostatic tachycardia syndrome (POTS), where heart rate increases quickly during orthostatic intolerance.[3,4,13] The tilt table is one way to diagnose orthostatic intolerance. During this test, a person lays on a table-like surface and is strapped in. The table is then tilted slowly upward to mimic movement from lying to standing. Blood flow is typically assessed using Doppler placed on the head. Heart rate and blood pressure, as indications of cardiac response, are measured too.

Many researchers have found reduced cerebral blood flow among those with CFS at the same time that they experience orthostatic intolerance. In Linda van Campen and team's recent study of 60 people with CFS, all experienced symptoms of orthostatic intolerance and reduced cerebral blood flow.[14] In addition, van Campen observed delayed return to normal blood flow in all participants. Further, the more severe their CFS symptoms, the slower the return to adequate blood distribution. The research, therefore, shows that impaired vascular constriction and dilation play an important role in CFS symptoms of Raynaud's and orthostatic intolerance. What about cognitive problems, another aspect of CFS?

Not only do those with CFS experience physical exhaustion, they encounter mental fatigue too. This shows up as memory and thinking problems or what's called brain fog. Some describe it like this: "Your thoughts become hard to see, you can't focus" (Sam);[15] I sometimes cannot even think . . . everything seems confusing to me at times and I can't make sense of it."[16]

We know now that those with CFS show inadequate blood distribution and flow or hypoperfusion to given brain areas.[14,17] Klaus Wirth and team offer a reason why blood hypoperfusion might affect cognition[18] - blood vessels intertwine closely with neurons (neurovascular coupling), so blood flow disruption means that these neurons don't get the fuel precursors and nutrients they need to operate properly. Noted earlier, ED affects lymphatic vessels too. Brain endothelium makes cerebrospinal fluid which then drains into the brain's lymphatic or glymphatic system.[19,20] Brain ED, then, disrupts not only blood flow but cerebrospinal fluid mechanics and thus the brain's waste removal system. The brain and spinal cord show high metabolism[20] so transporting material needed for metabolism and removing metabolic end-products are key to healthy central nervous system functioning. Disturbance of all these elements of brain and spinal cord endothelia may account for disrupted cognition. Interestingly, the glymphatic system functions mostly during sleep and this may explain why our ability to think clearly declines after a night of poor sleep. Poor sleep is another hallmark of CFS, but more on that later.

Another key job of the endothelium is to stabilize blood pressure. Because smaller arteries have more muscle, they have more control over blood flow and distribution than larger arteries. With more elastic fibers than muscle, larger vessels dominate control of tone and blood pressure. Elastic fibers surrounding vessels do this by stretching and recoiling.[5,6] Larger vessels situate closer to important organs such as the heart. Blood pressure is measured by looking at two numbers. The first is the amount of pressure used to pump blood out of the left ventricle, the main pumping chamber. This pressure, which forces the pumping chamber to contract, is systolic. The second number is the amount of pressure present when blood fills the left ventricle. This chamber dilates to aid filling and so the resulting pressure, diastolic, is typically lower than the systolic. Heart failure follows disruption of either type of pressure.[21] Diastolic heart failure results when the pumping chamber does not relax enough to fill well and so pressure increases (hypertension) to push out enough blood. Systolic heart failure results when there is not enough pressure (hypotension) to pump enough blood out of the pumping chamber. The result is inadequate blood output to the rest of the body.[21] While hypertension has long elicited concern, hypotension presents challenges too.[22]

Hypotension is common among those with CFS.[23-25] Many show relatively low diastolic pressure, however the big difference from the general population is the lower systolic pressure. What does this mean in terms of pumping chamber dilation and constriction? For the most part, chamber dilation and thus filling are adequate. The problem emerges when chamber pressure is too low during the process of squeezing blood out of it. Low pressure results in low constriction; less constriction results in less output. The amount of blood available for distribution body-wide is lower and so the endothelium compensates for this by altering blood flow dynamics. This shows up as a bias toward vessel narrowing in the periphery (i.e., hand, feet, brain) and a bias toward vessel relaxation among central organs.

The scenario above tells a large part of the story but not everything. Kidneys and adrenal glands control blood pressure too. They do this by controlling the amount of fluids and salts in the body. Known as the renin-angiotensin aldosterone system (RAAS), it manages blood volume.[26] When blood pressure is too low, the kidneys release renin which prompts angiotensin release which then prompts aldosterone release from the adrenal glands. Aldosterone then tells the kidneys to keep fluids in the body because more fluids increase blood pressure. In this scenario, aldosterone also directs cells to keep salts (sodium and potassium) because higher salt concentrations increase blood volume. When blood pressure is too high, the RAAS tries to reduce the volume of body fluids and salt concentrations. One way to do this is to increase urination. Many with CFS present with low blood volume (hypovolemia);[27] which implies that the RAAS may be challenged too. This, in turn, contributes toward problems with regulating blood pressure, adding to cardiac distress.[28] Let's, however, attempt to sum up cardiovascular involvement in CFS.

Many who experience CFS show one or a combination of conditions such as Raynaud's Syndrome, orthostatic intolerance, and cognitive disturbance. All can be traced to disrupted blood flow and distribution. Hypotension, particularly systolic hypotension, is part of the CFS picture. This can be traced to blood pressure disruption. Peripheral hypoperfusion and hypotension result from ED and so are early signals of heart disease. We know also that these cardiovascular irregularities present themselves among those with CFS. Early research by Leonard Jason and team[29] indicates that a large portion of those with CFS die from heart failure. Others have since confirmed this.[30-32] Given all these observations, it's hard to ignore the idea that cardiovascular operations play a significant role in CFS.

11. Chronic Fatigue Syndrome and the Nervous System

Sleep

Let's delve into another key symptom of CFS - poor sleep. What is the nature of sleep experienced by those with CFS? It is described by most as being non-restorative in that it is unrefreshing and poor quality, interrupted by episodes of wakefulness during the night, and then difficulty resuming sleep.[1-3] Sleep studies support these reports and indicate that those with CFS show reduced short-wave sleep and abnormal alpha and delta rhythms, which mean they wake up during NREM.[4,5] Resulting shallow sleep indicated by these experiences imply also elevated vigilance during sleep.

Such vigilance suggests that the sympathetic nervous system is relatively more active than the parasympathetic during sleep and many studies confirm this.[6] Heart rate variability, for instance, is lower;[5] systolic and mean blood pressure tend to be higher and heart rate tends to be lower.[7,8] A heightened sympathetic nervous system shows up as extreme sensitivity to external stimuli such as light and sound, and internal stimuli such as worries and intrusive thoughts. Such stimuli at night while trying to sleep often delay and disrupt sleep.[9] Others propose that poor sleep is due to altered immune system activity. Increased circulating pro-inflammatory cytokines (biochemicals released from immune cells) are to blame,[10] in particular IL-6.[5,11] Among those with CFS, irregular immune response shows up also in altered L-tryptophan levels, needed to make melatonin.[12]

Night-time awakenings are part of the poor sleep experience. Those with CFS show a different pattern of stage shifts than those without insomnia.[5] They tend to go from the first stage of NREM, the lightest sleep stage, back to wakefulness more often. This results in difficulty falling asleep and is due likely to enhanced sympathetic activity and thus vigilance noted above. In addition, those with CFS tend to wake up after REM instead of transitioning back to NREM.

During REM, the body uses more energy and becomes hotter than other stages. During NREM, however, core body and brain temperatures drop.[13,14] Interestingly, the same conditions precede arousal from torpor that hibernating creatures exhibit. The interbout arousal parallels stage shift during sleep. Overall, those with CFS have fewer REM to NREM shifts.[5] This stage shift difference is related likely to altered body temperature control since the body needs to cool down again to re-enter NREM.[14] Many with sleep problems experience extreme bodily heat or coldness during the night and report these temperature extremes as one reason for nighttime awakening.[15]

Researchers such as Pier Parmeggiani found that the body temperature regulation mechanism dials down a lot and maybe switches off during REM.[13] Most of us arrange our sleeping spaces so that we protect ourselves from extreme surrounding temperatures.[14] When it's too cold, for instance, we huddle under blankets or when it's too hot we might open windows. We are, in effect, creating a microenvironment around our bodies to attain and stabilize a tolerable environmental temperature. We do this because our internal temperature regulation mechanism seems to take a break during REM. Thus we set up our sleeping space to protect ourselves from extremes in surrounding temperature. It may well be that the purpose of REM is to rest the autonomic nervous system.

The autonomic nervous system controls body temperature. When we sleep, extreme body temperatures (hot and cold) jolt us into wakefulness which of course aids survival. Those with and without insomnia may differ by the mechanism used to jolt awakening, which happens rapidly in response to other stimuli too such as noise or touch. One possibility is that a startle response is triggered during sleep and this causes awakening. We know that those with CFS have lower circulating cortisol and thus lower adrenaline levels. Increased sensitivity to these substances means that a startle response is triggered more easily among those with sleep problems. Whereas those without insomnia continue to sleep through changes in body temperature or changes in external stimuli like sound or touch, those with insomnia can not. Once awakened, the body must go through the whole process of reducing body heat and return to a parasympathetic state. Then, as noted above, the body must dial down the temperature regulation mechanism so that we enter REM sleep. This in turn requires proper gamma aminobutyric acid (GABA) functioning.[16] GABA is the chief calming neurotransmitter of the central nervous system and is involved also in body temperature regulation.[16,17] Dysfunction here causes insomnia[18] because GABA helps to reduce[17] and maybe switch off the internal temperature control machine. Sleep problems experienced by those with CFS, therefore, are caused also by a glitch in GABA operations. Chronodisruption, experienced by many with CFS,[19,20] indicates such a glitch. Furthermore, persistent sleep difficulties indicate autonomic nervous system disruption.

Unsatisfactory sleep occurs most often during CFS flare-ups when other symptoms worsen. Similar to fatigue, poor sleep exerts many negative affects on activities of daily living, cognition and mood. Indeed, some with CFS believe that poor sleep is their worst symptom and many report that poor sleep makes all the other symptoms more challenging to manage.[2] In concert with this sentiment is the finding that pain experience and poor sleep overlap.[21,22] What's certain is that a good nights sleep alleviates pain[1] but poor sleep accentuates pain.[21,22]

Pain

Pain comprises another key symptom of CFS. Three categories occur: nociceptive, neuropathic, and nociplastic.[23-25] Nociceptive results from tissue inflammation and damage, neuropathic from neural injury and nociplastic from altered pain processing and experience. Nociplastic pain does not have obvious physical causes, covers broad areas of the body, features hypersensitivity and includes mood disturbance.[26,27] In addition, it persists over time, at least three months. Those with CFS experience all three types of pain to some degree with emphasis on neuropathic and nociplastic. Anxiety and depression are common in this group and could be viewed as being both neuropathic and nociplastic.

To determine why pain occurs, it is helpful to focus on the relatively unique features of pain experienced by those with

CFS: Body-wide, atypical biochemistry and enhanced sensitivity.[1,23] Pain that follows physical activity, even small amounts, results from musculoskeletal strain and extends all over the body. Body-wide achiness occurs also in the absence of any obvious activity. Slow- and fast-twitch muscles activate in both scenarios. Slow-twitch activate during prolonged stress mostly, exert low force and include those used to maintain posture.[28-30] They predominate the musculoskeletal make-up of the back, for instance, use fatty acids for fuel mostly, and rely on oxygen supply to make ATP. Consequently, they have many mitochondria. As the smallest muscle fiber in the body, slow-twitch store little glycogen and are innervated by smaller nerves and blood vessels, so interact with many capillaries and thus endothelia.

Fast-twitch activate during speed stress (usually brief), exert a lot of force and include those used to run and jump. They use glucose and store glycogen for energy, and engage anaerobic (no oxygen) respiration to make ATP. Fast-twitch are bigger than slow-twitch and predominate the lower limbs. Note that slow- and fast-twitch differ in how they make ATP;

slow-twitch muscles rely on oxygen whereas fast-twitch don't. The body responds to stress by altering blood flow and thus oxygen and nutrient availability. Inadequate oxygen supply (hypoxia) and nutrients, therefore, affect slow-twitch muscles initially. Now, they have to resort to more anaerobic respiration and make other mitochondrial adjustments. Under suboptimal conditions, the same muscles have to exert more force to do the same work. As Riyad El-Khoury and team[31] point out, when more force is needed, muscle fatigue follows. The same team found that after about six weeks of chronic hypoxia, both muscle types change and become fatigued more easily. In addition, levels of lactate, hydrogen ions, free adenosine diphosphate (ADP) and adenosine monophosphate (AMP) increase. The increase of these biochemicals imply a shift in mitochondrial operations and pain amplification;[32] together, they signal fatigue and then pain. When Cara Tomas and team[33] examined skeletal muscle from those with CFS, they found differences in how cellular energy was made compared to those without CFS. The difference lay in how the mitochondria work. Although comparable levels of ATP are made, the mechanism for using oxygen (called OXPHOS) disrupts in those with CFS. Further research by Paula Fernandez-Guerra and team[34] show that mitochondrial disruption centers on how two biochemicals are used, acetyl co-enzyme A and pyruvate dehydrogenase. Both are key to making ATP and both are disturbed in CFS.[34,35] Regarding pain, the important point here is that chronic stress affects muscles body-wide. In addition, fast-twitch muscles require longer recovery time[29] so pain in these muscle fibers persists longer than in slow-twitch. Further, such conditions likely increase pain sensitivity due to increased circulation of more pain-related biochemicals.

Other important elements of CFS contribute to enhanced pain. One is reduced cortisol which presents in CFS.[4,20,36] Not only is cortisol anti-inflammatory, it prompts noradrenaline release, which too reduces pain.[36] Blunted cortisol release nudges the body toward a pro-inflammatory state, which amplifies inflammatory immune responses that cause pain too.

What about neuropathic pain? Many with CFS experience this in peripheral nerves. When peripheral blood vessels are prone to frequent constriction (due to an over-active sympathetic nervous system), a characteristic of CFS, they become vulnerable to hypoxia. Chronic hypoxic conditions affect endothelial function too. Specifically, availability of nitric oxide (NO) declines and results in super-oxide formation.[37] In turn, this places oxidative stress on the endothelium that eventually causes damage which is then sensed by the nerves that surround it. Subsequently, endothelial damage contributes to neuropathic pain.[38] Tissue damage activates also an immune response which likely intensifies pain sensation. Klaus Wirth and team[40] note that excessive vasoconstriction triggers release of vasodilators, such as bradykinin, which cause inflammation and elicit pain.[41] In sum, neuropathic pain and endothelial dysfunction go hand-in-hand. Next and finally, let us discuss aspects of nociplastic pain particularly depression.

12. Chronic Fatigue Syndrome and Depression

The wretchedness of chronic physical pain magnifies when mood-related pain, such as anxiety and depression coexist. Now viewed as important elements of nociplastic pain,[1] mood disturbance impacts almost every aspect of daily living. As social beings, chronic and extreme anxiety and depression debilitate in far-reaching ways our relationships with others and the ability to engage in fulfilling occupation and recreation, all elements of satisfactory living. Both mood disturbances are common to CFS.[2-4] Chronic anxiety is related to an over-active sympathetic and under-active parasympathetic nervous system. It shows up in the startle response and other signs of extreme fear. Some with CFS, however, say that continuous exhaustion and depression override and dampen anxious responses including startle. CFS symptoms, such as poor sleep, worsen anxiety. Work by Eti

Ben Simon and Matthew Walker, indicates that sleep reduces anxiety by about 30%.[5] Thus the enhanced vigilance that underlies poor sleep disrupts an important antidote for anxiety and perpetuates the dissatisfactory sleep cycle. Below, however, the focus is on chronic depression due to the chilling finding that suicide is a leading cause of death among those with CFS.[6-8] In some cases, extreme anxiety precipitates suicide, but depression is a major cause of suicide.

Depression associates with at least three elements of psychophysiological defense: the sympathovagal response, the HPA axis response, and the immune response. Together, these impact cardiovascular functioning. Regarding sympathovagal response, signs of disruption include dysautonomia and insomnia, both highly prevalent among those with CFS.[9,10] Evidence of HPA axis disruption displays in altered hormone levels and biorhythms. Relatively lower levels of cortisol and higher vasopressin levels have been found among those with increased suicide risk.[11] All of these conditions present in those with CFS to some degree. Regarding immune function, relatively high levels of pro-inflammatory biochemicals hallmark CFS. Key categories are reactive oxygen species, reactive nitrogen species, and cytokines such as tumor-necrosis factor alpha, and IL-6.[12-14] Behaviorally and psychologically, depression shows up as reduced social, occupational, and physical activity, loss of interest in pleasurable pursuits, and altered thinking and emotional expression.[15]

Regarding the cardiovascular response, heart disease and depression go hand-in-hand. Among those with heart failure, for instance, about 22% to 30% experience major depression.[16-18] This figure increases to about 50% when we consider depression symptoms such as fatigue, sleep problems, and low quality of life.[18] Large-scale heart disease studies, such as the TRIUMPH Registry[19] and Emerging Risk Factors Collaboration,[20] confirm this association. Work by Seongkum Heo,[21] shows that depression and heart failure not only go together, but the more symptoms of heart failure experienced, the worse the emotional (depression and anxiety) experiences too. Lack of clarity exists, however, on what comes first - heart damage or depression? Pondering this question, Robert

Dantzer notes,[22] "The possibility that depression is not just a disorder of the mind but rather a consequence of physical illness has haunted medicine for a long time." Accumulating evidence indicates the latter may be true. Moreover, among those with CFS, who experience both conditions, the belief here is that cardiovascular disturbance causes depression. We will explore this idea next.

For a long time, scientists believed that the brain directed human behavior including heart operations along a one-way path of communication. James Armour[23] and Julian Thayer's work,[24] however, indicates that this goes both ways with the heart communicating to the brain too: indeed, there's far more neural communication from the heart to brain. This implies that the heart also directs human behavior, maybe more than we know.

In a prospective study, where people were followed over time, Jay Patel and team discovered that certain factors increased the odds of developing depression.[25] Not only did they find that the cardiovascular disease risk factors of obesity and tobacco use predicted depression, but that hypertension predicted it too. Hypertension is an adaptive cardiovascular response to physical distress. Altered blood lipids are another cardiovascular disease predictor. Siyao Zhou and team[26] link major depression and suicidal behavior to increased total blood cholesterol, triglycerides, and low density lipoprotein-c together with low levels of high density lipoprotein-c. They report also that positive changes in these lipid levels can occur with physical training and this change improves signs of depression.

Along another line of research, heart problems cause cognitive problems such as memory loss and confusion.[27,28] Michiaki Nagai and team localize cognitive disturbances to the insular cortex.[29,30] This brain part is involved in processing incoming sensory information, emotions, risk-reward behavior, pain and autonomic functioning. Nagai and team note that insular cortex location surrounded by middle cerebral arteries makes it vulnerable to cerebrovascular disease. Blood flow problems, therefore, likely exert a strong impact on this brain area. They observe also that heart muscle injury links to insular cortex damage. One way this shows up is in sympathetic over-activity, a condition common to many with CFS. In addition, Eric Ichesco and team,[31] provide evidence that the insular cortex behaves differently in those with CFS compared to those who don't have CFS. Pain perception involves connections between the insular and cingulate cortices. Among those with CFS, more of these connections are evident. Further, the denser these connections the more pain experienced. Insular cortex alterations have been observed among adolescents with CFS too.[32]

From the world of surgery, we know that heart surgery, which incurs physical trauma to heart tissue, causes brain injury.[33] Agreeing with Nagai and team, Rongian Zou and colleagues[33] note that the insular cortex which they consider the area of cardiac perception, is particularly sensitive. They suspect that one cause of injury comes from free floating particles (emboli) that form in heart vessels during surgery and later block brain blood vessels. Brain injury occurs also from inflammation and reduced brain blood perfusion. The first sign of brain damage may be a drop in blood pressure following cardiac surgery and this has been observed.[34] Going further,

Daijiro Hori and team[35] tracked blood pressure and assessed brain damage by looking at specific protein levels (i.e., glial fibrillary acidic proteins) among patients who had cardiac surgery. Although glial fibrillary proteins were elevated in all patients following surgery, they were higher among those with lower blood pressure and cerebral oxygen. Also, they found that the less blood pumped out the more brain injury observed. In sum, heart trauma causes brain trauma. The ability to reason and respond emotionally in a manner that promotes engagement and survival versus hopelessness and suicide is a cognitive-emotional response. Heart trauma can diminish this ability.

Another avenue of thought that indicates cardiac cause of depression comes from the kidney's role in controlling blood pressure. Low blood pressure stimulates at least three responses to elevate it. First, vasopressin (in brain) increases blood volume since it directs the kidneys to keep fluid in the body. Relatively high vasopressin levels are seen in those with depression.[11,36] In addition, low blood pressure stimulates the adrenal gland to release aldosterone which tells the kidney to retain salts. Salt retention elevates blood pressure. Finally, the kidneys release renin which helps to make angiotensin II, a vasoconstrictor that increases blood pressure. Interestingly, blocking vasoconstriction appears to improve depression.[37] Drugs which do this are known as angiotensin converting enzyme (ACE) inhibitors. Why would they have this effect?

Let's return to the topic of inflammation. Dantzer and team were among the first to link inflammation outside the brain and spinal cord to altered brain responding.[22] They, and others, reasoned that if immune activation can make us feel sick then it can also make us feel depressed. Digging deeper, Dantzer and team noticed other relationships.[38] People with cancer and hepatitis C who were treated with immunotherapy became depressed. Because immunotherapy enhances defensive immune cell responses, it stimulates immune cells to release pro-inflammatory cytokines. Examples of these include interferon N alpha and IL-2. Although released outside the central nervous system, these cytokines targeted brain tissue too, particularly the prefrontal cortex implicated in depression. The same region showed hypometabolism and altered glucose metabolism, both of these are associated with torpor or repair. Further, people in this condition reported higher states of depression and fatigue.

In their review of neurocognitive disorders after heart failure, Camilo Toledo and team[39] propose a mechanism for how this might happen. It works like this: heart tissue damage causes emboli to form that later block brain blood vessels that either impede blood flow or trigger inflammation. In addition, or alternatively, because heart failure lowers blood output, it lowers brain blood flow too. The ensuing lack of life-supporting resources causes neuronal injury and possibly death. Both scenarios trigger release of pro-inflammatory substances because damaged and dead cells activate the brain's defensive immune response. Chengyang Xu's team,[28] suggests that increases in TNF-alpha and IL-1 beta provoke this chain of pro-inflammatory events causing also excessive glutamate release, a known neurotoxin when it gathers outside cells.[40] Recently, researchers discovered that ketamine, which tamps down glutamate action, improves depression in a quick and fairly dramatic manner.[41]

Now, let's return to ACE inhibitors. As the name suggests, these drugs block angiotensin II from entering cells. ACE inhibitors lower heart contraction activity and so increase heart muscle relaxation and thus blood vessel widening. Crucially, this improves blood availability to the brain. Not only does this aid nutrient and oxygen delivery, it assists also in waste disposal, a key element of repair. The simple explanation, therefore, is that ACE inhibitors effect improvement by restoring brain blood flow and distribution. On a related sidenote, drugs for erectile dysfunction, which improve blood flow too, appear to improve symptoms of Alzheimer's.[42]

Let's relate the observations above to CFS. We can agree, at this point, that many with CFS show early signs of heart muscle damage.[43-45] In addition, they show cognitive disturbance and experience anxiety and depression. Heart damage is associated with metabolic shift. During good health, mitochondria in cardiomyocytes use fatty acids mostly for biofuel. According to research by Julia Ritterhoff and Rong Tian,[46] damaged hearts switch to using more glucose and ketones. While this switch maintains ATP supply, it does so at a cost when energy demand increases under stressful conditions.[47] Under chronic distress, this shift becomes more permanent because the mitochondria remodel to adapt.[48] Such remodeling, however, results in reduced flexibility to use other types of fuel such as fatty acids. Sustained reliance on glucose and ketones for fuel eventually damage mitochondria. As Bo Zhou and Rong Tian put it,[47] "they become failed power plants." The failing power plant is now more vulnerable to calcium overload that causes the mitochondrial wall to break and release inner material. This material includes cytochrome C, ROS, and mitochondrial DNA [mtDNA], all of which signal and trigger cell death. But this is not all because these biochemicals, once outside the cell, activate the innate immune response. Mitochondrial DNA, in particular, does this by prompting inflammasomes into action.

Excessive, prolonged distress whether generated internally or externally, causes a metabolic shift in heart muscles. The shift eventually damages mitochondria that then activate an immune response. Recall, immune cells respond to cellular injury. Under chronic distress, the metabolic shift becomes more permanent leading to inefficient cardiomyocyte function over time; this means that the pumping chamber does not pump enough oxygenated blood and nutrients to critical organs like the brain. This in turn causes hypoxic and ischemic episodes and later inflammation that affect the insular cortex.[49] Over time, the insular cortex adjusts to altered blood flow and begins to direct the heart and thus the rest of the body to slow down or to depress activity. Although the heart and brain communicate in a bidirectional manner, initial disturbance begins in disturbed heart and blood vessels.

In sum, heart muscle damage causes cerebral hypoperfusion which changes the insular cortex and disrupts cognitive functioning. We know now that many with CFS die from heart failure or suicide, the ultimate consequence of depression. The conclusion here is that heart muscle damage prompts depression. And death follows from either the damage that leads to heart failure or from the severe depression that heart injury instigates.

13. Promising Treatment Approaches

In repair mode, we experience fatigue, poor sleep, and negative mood. A key idea here is that these disturbances signal cardiovascular disturbance. Specifically, the autonomic nervous system of the heart disrupts following chronic distress whether such distress is caused by pathogenic infection or psychophysiological trauma.[1] It shows up as dysautonomia - too much or too little sympathetic and parasympathetic neural activity. Dysautonomia results in widespread disruption to many activities we do unconsciously, such as: blood pressure regulation, body temperature control, and immune cell responses. Further, dysautonomia precedes and accompanies many illnesses such as cardiovascular disease[2,3] and diabetes.[4] Treatment approaches that improve dysautonomia, therefore, improve cardiovascular wellness too which ripple out to better sleep, mood, and bioenergetics. Below we explore this idea further.

Can the cardiac autonomic nervous system be reset? Yes, and we examine two approaches here. One method improves heart rate variability (HRV) and is based on the concept of coherence. The other, called stellate ganglion block, alters sympathetic communication between the heart and the brain. Psychophysiological coherence is harmonious connectedness within and across body systems.[5] According to the HeartMath Institute, health is the ability to maintain coherence.[5,6] The heart has enough nervous tissue that it is seen as having its own brain, called the heart-brain.[7] If you recall, the heart sends more messages to the brain than the brain sends to the heart. So it is a major sensory organ in addition to being an effector organ. In fact, coherence researchers believe that the heart generates emotions and the ability to manage them is central to wellbeing.[5,6] Their work shows that improving emotional regulation improves autonomic function and this improves thinking and behaving.[6,8-13]

The hallmark of coherence is a smooth HRV rhythm with numerical values that reflect a pattern of heartbeat flexibility. Similar patterns emerge when we experience positive emotions like love. Incoherence, on the other hand, manifests as a jagged rhythm and low HRV. The same pattern emerges during unwanted emotions like frustration. The goal of coherence therapy, therefore, is to teach the autonomic nervous system of the heart to operate in a way that enhances sympathovagal balance, improves organ synchrony, and assists effective operation of our stress response systems such as the immune cells and HPA axis.[5,6]

HeartMath researchers have developed a few techniques and computer applications (apps) toward accomplishing this goal. These techniques share important components such as tuning breathing rate to the same one engaged during coherence, shifting attention to the heart and imagining breath entering and leaving it, and evoking positive emotions and thoughts to strengthen coherence.[5,6] Together, these elements harness the power of emotional regulation to improve wellbeing and positive effects have been experienced among many including students,[8,14] military personnel,[9,10] police,[11] pilots,[12] and those with medical conditions like hypertension,[15] PTSD,[10] and congestive heart failure.[16] Further, increased coherence improves sleep,[17] mood,[9,11-13] and fatigue.[13] Interestingly, those who practice yoga techniques of meditation, posture, and breath control show vagal activity and baroreflex sensitivity levels consistent with coherence.[18]

Increasing coherence uses accessible tactics such as managing breathing and evoking positive emotional states, however, stellate ganglion block (SGB) is a surgical procedure;[19] though less invasive approaches are used too.[20] The stellate ganglion, a cluster of sympathetic nerve bodies with long fibers, connects the heart to the hypothalamus, insula, and amygdala - all involved in responses we make automatically such as threat detection. Under chronic distress, this bundle of nerves becomes more active: new nerves sprout, the cell body cluster enlarges, and nerve connection density increases.[21] Together, these changes enhance sympathetic responding. Eugene Lipov and team found that blocking this neural highway reduces sympathetic activity and improves associated symptoms.[19] The nerve is blocked by injecting a local, long acting anesthetic into the stellate ganglion next to the voice box in the neck. Employed originally, as far back as the 1920s, to ease pain,[22] SGB helps to reduce ventricular arrhythmias,[21] hot flashes,[19] and PTSD symptoms.[22,23] One of the almost immediate effects of SGB is improved blood flow to the head and hands.[24] This supports the earlier observation that too much sympathetic activity impedes peripheral blood flow. While Lipov acknowledges that this outcome adds to symptom improvement, he believes that the block works because it causes an epigenetic shift that rebalances stellate ganglion responding in a fairly permanent way.[25] The epigenetic shift itself is likely a switch to a different biodefense that relies less on sympathetic arousal. Much of recent SGB research has been done with military personnel who experience PTSD and chronic pain. Using HRV biofeedback training, Melanie Berry and team report improvement in pain, perceived stress, negative emotions, and physical activity limitations among those with chronic pain.[9] Regarding

PTSD, SGB improves anxiety and many other symptoms associated with PTSD.[22]

An important point here is that our predisposition to entrain allows some flexibility in that we can adjust our responses to the life rhythms that we function within. In other words, we can reset our biological rhythms to optimize health. This knowledge underlies some of the relatively new approaches to treating chronic disease. Eating patterns can be reset by fasting or restricted feeding.[26,27] The latter involves eating during specific time periods only and not eating for relatively long gaps of time, from about 12 to 16 hours. Not only does this technique help weight loss, it improves markers of chronic disease.[28,29] Blood levels of glucose, insulin, and triglycerides, for instance, improve. Further, dietary change is a powerful way to enhance health. Leveraging the healing ability of the microbiome, Terry Wahls advocates massive increases in green vegetable intake.[30] And this approach works, certainly for those with multiple sclerosis. A fairly new way to address depression is to reset sleeping patterns. Pioneered by Francesco Bernadetti,[31] this method requires participants to remain awake through an entire daily cycle or longer. Although positive effects are almost immediate, they don't endure. For this reason extended wakefulness is being paired with bright-light therapy and supplements such as lithium to prolong benefits. Such tweaking appears to be more successful than extended wakefulness alone.[32]

The use of bright light exposure for health is not new and associates mostly with treatment for seasonal affective disorder (SADS). With this condition, people experience depression as days become shorter with less light and warmth.[33] SADS begins generally in the fall and continues on during winter. Those who live in the Arctic experience such conditions for an even longer duration. Not everyone there develops SADS, but many show changes in sleeping patterns, mood, and immune cell behavior.[34,35] To counter prolonged darkness, artificial bright light is used.[35] Adding bright light exposure during morning hours helps those working in extreme environments to cope with low to no sunlight.[36] In sum, biorhythm reset, whether the disruption is with feeding, activity levels, or sleeping patterns, is both doable and beneficial. Leveraging knowledge about biorhythms underpins the field of chronomedicine.

14. Chapter Summaries

1. The Nature of Threat and Defense

The defense cascade shows the sequence of defense behaviors used following acute threat. Defense is activated via the autonomic nervous system which is part of the central nervous system. Our biological defense mechanisms express themselves both internally and externally. Freezing or running, for example, appears externally as whole-body behavior. Traditionally, the immune cell response was considered the dominant mechanism of internal biodefense. We are learning, however, that internal biodefense is more complex and invokes neurologically prompted actions in concert with, for instance, immune cell, cardiovascular, and endocrine systems. The defense cascade describes a sequence of behaviors that occur in response to acute danger but what happens when threat becomes chronic?

Torpor and hibernation are likely activated in response to chronic threat and are periods during which repair occurs. Using the example of seasonal cycle, many nonhuman creatures are more active and healthier during spring and summer. As threat becomes chronic, however, they become less active and healthy and repair dominates life. Torpor represents the short-term version of repair while hibernation is a longer repair cycle. How we engage psychophysiological repair links to personal patterns of defense. Humans appear to engage facultative torpor for organ repair. Since torpor and hibernation show cyclical features then internal defense likely operates in a cyclical manner too. In turn, this observation means that health has cyclical elements and research has been confirming this. Understanding human health, therefore, requires an understanding of important ideas such as biorhythms, environmental rhythms, dominant life tasks, torpor and hibernation, and the nature of humans' psychophysiological response to distress.

2. Biorhythms

Two forces influence how we engage life tasks: environmental signals such as light and temperature and internal signals such as biofuel and hormone levels. Biorhythms generate internally and humans show many; daily and monthly biorhythms being the most familiar. Cortisol, insulin and melatonin, for instance show daily or circadian rhythms that align with the life tasks of activity, feeding, and repair or growth. Environmental signals come from the earth rotating the sun and include daily or diurnal changes in light and temperature. Humans are sensitive to these signals and entrain to them.

The biological mechanism that allows alignment between circadian and diurnal rhythms is the brain-based suprachiasmatic nucleus (SCN). Known also as the master clock, the SCN coordinates action across peripheral clocks. Such "time-keeping" allows also coordination across life tasks. Chronodisruption occurs in two ways. One, when our biorhythms don't align with environmental ones and two, when peripheral clocks don't align with the SCN. Both states indicate illness.

Biorhythms show several features: periodicity, wave patterns with peaks and troughs, amplitude, repetition, nesting, are fractal, and can be reset. Junwen Guan's work showed that in humans, shorter cycles exert more influence than longer ones. However, during trauma, longer cycles kick in likely to lengthen and aid repair. Repair cycles that extend beyond the circadian parallel hibernation. Guan's findings indicate that humans enter such states when extensive psychophysiological repair is needed. This can show up as chronodisruption, which means that healthy growth stalls as the body tries to fix damage. This state is common to many chronic diseases. Chronomedicine addresses biological dysynchrony and operates from the premise that treatment timing is an important element of recovery.

3. Life Tasks

The cell growth cycle is fundamental to life and proceeds through three subcycles that can be characterized as tasks. Through this lens, resource gathering and conversion, which occur during interphase comprise the first two tasks. Before the third task - growth, there is a quality control pause.

Growth proceeds only if quality criteria such as intact DNA, are met. Benjamin Tu and team's work showed that yeast colonies engaged three sub-cycles or tasks: resource accumulation, growth and repair. Each subcycle shows its own metabolic rate and epigenetic signature. They showed that subcycles are sequential and that cellular growth aligns with metabolic task.

Because they last a long time relative to other cell types, terminally differentiated cells need longer repair time. If the circadian cycle can not provide this then repair likely shifts into the next longer one, maybe seven days. When this happens with humans, chronodisruption results. The body may then show signs of adjusted biorhythms, torpor, or even organ hibernation. Evidence of this include altered neurohormonal biorhythms, altered sleep patterns and chronic fatigue.

4. Hibernation

Hibernation looks like this: exit external environment, prepare nest, adjust posture, subdue activity, slow breathing, tamp down metabolism and reduce basal body temperature. This state poses danger due to starvation, muscle wasting, and reduced immune cell activity. Hibernators address starvation by relying on internally stored fatty acids with the added benefit of bypassing the gastrointestinal system and giving it time to rest. To minimize muscle waste, protein breakdown balances with protein production, anti-oxidant and anti-nitrosative biochemicals and gases increase, protective protein levels go up and muscle tissue restructures itself.

Although immune defense drops, the hibernatory state itself confers protection since isolation, colder body temperature, less feeding by mouth, and reduced breathing decrease odds of injury by predator, pathogen, radiation or other environmental contaminants. The same changes make internal conditions inhospitable for existing pathogens and possibly eliminate them or impede colonization. Instead, immune cells shift focus to recycling or clearing damaged material. Blood flow changes too via a decline in rate, composition and distribution. All these changes assist pathogen control or elimination and reduce waste build-up. In sum, a hibernating body shows what extended psychophysiological repair looks like.

5. Sleep

Sleep is a subcycle of the circadian and hibernation is a subcycle of the circannual biorhythm. Sleep, therefore, is a smaller fractal of hibernation. They parallel each other across many variables. First, the main purpose of both is repair and, for some, growth. They share similar proportions in relation to the cycles to which they belong, that is comprising about a third of such cycles. They share also NREM and REM patterns, brain activity patterns (electroencephalograms), and the sequence through which these patterns activate in the brain.

Biochemicals central to both sleep and hibernation include melatonin, adenosine, and gamma aminobutyric acid (GABA). Melatonin, increases during both sleep and hibernation. This coincides with its role as anti-antioxidant and the shift toward anti-oxidant and anti-nitrosative defense observed during sleep and hibernation. In this role, melatonin protects against reperfusion injury due to fluctuating organ (especially the brain) blood flow during sleep and torpor. Alternatively, adenosine declines during the night and increases during daytime. This coincides with its role in making ATP, which gets used up with daytime activity and is replenished at night. Adenosine plays a key role also in stimulating sleep and torpor onset. GABA works with adenosine to induce both sleep and torpor. As an abundant nerve relaxant, GABA increases in the evening to peak at night. GABA levels increase during hibernation too. GABA is a key suprachiasmatic nucleus messenger and aids sleep onset by coordinating sleep across organ clocks so that the whole body sleeps in unison. One way it exerts this effect is through thermoregulation. GABA prevents the body from engaging cold defense and thus sets up the conditions for entry into the NREM portion of sleep and torpor.

Chronic sleep disruption signals illness and may indicate organ shift into a repair period longer than that provided by sleep. Given the similarities between sleep and hibernation, it is likely that chronodisrupted organs shift into a hibernatory state of extended repair.

6. Internal Distress

Our holobiomes consist of billions of microbes including bacteria, protozoa, viruses and fungi that live with us and help with the tasks of resource gathering, resource conversion, and repair or growth. When healthy, our immune cells and holobiomes cooperate to protect our bodies. Sometimes, microbes, whether they are part of the holobiome or arrive from the external environment, endanger us due to overgrowth or translocation to body parts that are not their natural homes.

Such infections trigger a resistant immune cell response that tries to control or get rid of the pathogen. The fighting stance adopted by immune cells, however, eventually causes collateral tissue damage. Such destruction eventually re-orients immune cells toward a state of tolerance. Tolerance means that T cells in particular stop responding to the pathogen and biochemicals that it releases. The resulting anti-inflammatory orientation of immune cells allows repair.

Tolerance, however, gives pathogens who have survived initial attack an opportunity to gain a foothold in the human host. This is known as persistence. On re-infection with the same pathogen, symptoms and tissue damage can worsen. Pathogen persistence, therefore, causes chronic internal distress and creates conditions for autoimmunity to develop. In turn, the body switches into prolonged repair subcycles similar to hibernation.

7. Chronic Distress

Chronic distress impacts neural, endocrine and immune cells. Regarding neural cells, the autonomic nervous system disrupts resulting in dysautonomia. One demonstration of this is over-activation of the sympathetic and under-activation of the parasympathetic systems. Termed sympathovagal imbalance, this condition is reflected in relatively low HRV values, symptoms like orthostatic intolerance, and altered levels of adrenaline and noradrenaline.

Regarding endocrine function, the hypothalamic-pituitary-adrenal (HPA) axis activates upon increased need for biofuel resulting in increased cortisol, adrenaline, and noradrenaline. Together they increase blood glucose production and circulation, induce increased heart pumping and breathing, and increase ATP. Too many cortisol surges eventually results in downregulation of glucocorticoid and adrenergic receptors. This in turn increases pain experience, inflammation, and fatigue.

Immune cells respond also to a disrupted HPA system. As cortisol goes up, for instance, circulating innate immune cells retreat and levels of circulating effector T cells and natural killer cells drop. In other words, innate and adaptive immunity suppress. When cortisol levels are too low, however, then both innate and adaptive immunity are more active. The blunted cortisol levels seen in many chronic disease states biases the body toward a more pro-inflammatory state.

Altered immune cell behavior results in chronic inflammation that displays as prolonged periods of tolerance and resistance. In this situation, symptom flare-ups alternate with reduced symptom expression. If we can't return to a low-stress state long enough to restore properly then future responses to distress are compromised. The resulting bias toward pro-inflammatory responses amplifies vulnerability to chronic disease and other threats.

8. Chronic Distress and the Heart

Acute distress disrupts the cardiac autonomic nervous system and causes events such as takotsubo, viewed as temporary heart failure. Since sympathovagal balance disrupts, it may be viewed too as temporary dysautonomia. Chronic distress appears to nudge cardiomyocytes into hypometabolism. Cardiomyocytes have the most mitochondria in the body and they direct the drop in metabolism. Also, mitochondria switch from using fatty acids mostly for biofuel to using glucose and ketones.

Although the metabolic shift may be adaptive initially, prolonged hypometabolism results in metabolic inflexibility. Such a change in mitochondrial operations may signal also reorientation toward antioxidant production as a response to inflammatory, hypoxic, or ischemic threat. Moreover, continued use of glucose and ketones damages mitochondria and triggers an inflammatory immune response that results in cardiovascular disease. In this scenario, parts of the heart may enter extended repair periods that look like torpor or eventually, hibernation.

A sick heart shows up behaviorally in a few ways, however, fatigue is a key sign. The same symptom is central to a well-known yet elusive condition called, among other names, chronic fatigue syndrome (CFS). Given this observation, the premise here is that the fatigue experienced during CFS is due likely to heart disease. Although commonly used biomarkers, such as troponin levels, may not detect heart trouble, fatigue is an early clue to this condition.

9. Chronic Fatigue Syndrome

Chronic fatigue plays a central role in CFS. Other symptoms are: pain, insomnia, illness after physical exertion, and depression. CFS looks a lot like torpor and behavioral evidence to support this contention includes retreat from social and occupational activity, reduced physical activity, altered sleep patterns, and depressed mood. Metabolomic profile studies suggest mitochondrial shift to hypometabolism and possible mitochondrial damage. Signs of this include inflammation (pro) and elevated levels of hydrogen sulfide, reactive oxygen species (ROS) and reactive nitrogen species (RNS).

If the metabolic shift is an adaptation to chronic distress, whether internally or externally generated, then "toxin" production may be an attempt to control pathogens or adapt to an altered biological environment. Some of the relatively unusual symptoms of CFS, such as hypersensitivity to toxins, suggest disrupted adrenal gland function. Evidence of dysautonomia and autoimmunity indicate disrupted autonomic and immune responses. Immune cell attack of adrenergic receptors, especially those in heart tissue, implicate cardiovascular involvement in CFS. Such findings align with the idea that fatigue, a major symptom of CFS, signals heart trouble. In addition, mitochondrial disruption and elevated ROS and RNS exert a disproportionate effect on heart muscle functioning given the abundance of mitochondria in this tissue.

Regarding CFS, therefore, neural, hormonal, and immune responses show disturbance. Mitochondrial disruption and elevated toxins seem to explain such disturbance. Extreme immune disturbance shows up as autoimmunity and those with CFS show a few different types of autoimmunity.

10. Chronic Fatigue Syndrome and the Cardiovascular System

Endothelial dysfunction (ED) predicts heart disease. Among those with CFS, ED shows up in Raynaud Syndrome, orthostatic intolerance, and cognitive problems. Raynaud's results from poor blood distribution to hands and feet which become cold and sometimes stiff. Although reversible, Raynaud's can be painful and is associated with eventual death due to heart disease. Orthostatic intolerance, the experience of illness upon changing body position or prolonged standing, represents another sign of ED. The preceding state of reduced peripheral blood distribution makes postural adjustment difficult to achieve or prolonged standing difficult to maintain. Symptoms include dizziness, nausea, and blurred vision. Cognitive disturbance, which displays as poor memory and thinking problems, can be caused by ED. In this scenario, ED results in brain hypoperfusion (a drop in brain blood flow and distribution), observed among some with CFS. Hypoperfusion means that brain tissue does not get adequate oxygen and nutrients and waste removal slows down causing waste accumulation.

Endothelia help to stabilize blood pressure, especially those in large vessels close to the heart. Disruptions here can cause inadequate contraction of the left ventricle which triggers hypertension. Blood pressure increases to help squeeze out enough blood and shows up as elevated systolic blood pressure. Alternatively, the left ventricle does not relax enough to fill properly thus triggering hypotension. This shows up as relatively low diastolic blood pressure. When blood pressure irregularities develop, the renin angiotensin aldosterone system (RAAS) of the adrenals and kidneys kick in. This system tries to stabilize blood pressure by altering blood volume. When volume is too low, the RAAS tries to retain body fluid by, for example, reducing urination.

Those with CFS are more likely to die from heart failure than the general population. The relatively high prevalence of conditions caused by endothelial dysfunction among those with CFS, strengthens the link between cardiovascular disease and CFS.

11. Chronic Fatigue Syndrome and the Nervous System

Three other significant CFS symptoms are: sleep disturbance, amplified pain, and depression. Together they indicate neural disruption. Sleep and pain are addressed here and depression is discussed in the next chapter. Those with CFS show shallow sleep marked by enhanced vigilance. They are sensitive to external stimuli indicating sympathetic nervous system over-activity and show also differences in sleep stage shifts. One example of this is difficulty resuming sleep after waking. Temperature dysregulation, another indication of autonomic imbalance, accounts for stage shift irregularity. Dysfunctional GABA operations that prevent relaxation of cold defense responses help to explain temperature dysregulation. The latter coincides with chronodisruption, observed among those with CFS.

Those with CFS experience all three pain types to some extent, that is, nociceptive, neuropathic, and nociplastic. Pain is body-wide, and shows enhanced sensitivity and atypical biochemistry. The body-wide feature indicates slow-twitch muscle involvement. Because they rely on oxygen for energy generation, low oxygen conditions (hypoxia) affect these first.

Now, they have to work harder to execute the same responses such as maintaining posture. More effort results in fatigue and pain. Fast twitch muscles, however, are affected too. Under chronic hypoxic conditions, they too have to work harder to complete tasks like running. In turn, this is experienced as fatigue and then pain. Pain amplifies also due to reduced cortisol and the pro-inflammatory state that follows. Endothelial dysfunction contributes toward pain too.

12. Chronic Fatigue Syndrome and Depression

Depression is another important sign of CFS and can be viewed as a type of pain, nociplastic. One element of this is the lack of obvious physical causes, however, here the idea is that heart damage causes depressed mood. A state of chronic and enhanced defense shows up as altered functioning in: sympathovagal balance, the HPA axis, and immune cell responses. Those with CFS experience disruption in these areas indicated by dysautonomia, low cortisol, and altered adrenaline and noradrenaline levels, and relatively high levels of pro-inflammatory biochemicals.

The idea that heart damage causes depression comes from a few observations. First, heart disease and depression occur together across many disease types and the worse the heart damage, the more depression is experienced. Second, factors that predict heart disease are similar to those that predict depression. Hypertension, for instance, predicts both heart disease and depression. A third point is that heart damage causes brain damage. Cognitive problems are known to develop after heart surgery, for example, and compromised reasoning and thinking abilities are part of depression.

Another line of evidence comes from research that shows improved heart health improves depression too. Finally, there is a plausible explanation for how heart health affects mood. Heart damage reduces blood flow and distribution to the brain. Reduced blood flow means less oxygen and nutrients are delivered. Repeated episodes of this eventually cause cell damage and death, which activate the immune system. Immune cells in fighter mode create pro-inflammatory conditions that increase the odds of depressed behavior. When the brain is threatened and activates defense, it changes the type of biofuel it uses. This switch, if prolonged, can damage mitochondria and add to pro-inflammatory conditions. A notable finding consistent with the points above is that the main causes of death among those with CFS are heart failure and suicide.

13. Promising Treatment Approaches

Chronic distress shows up as dysautonomia, imbalance between parasympathetic and sympathetic nervous system functioning. The cardiac autonomic nervous system bears initial impact most. Blood pressure control, for example, engages early to counter disruptive effects. Two approaches show promise in addressing dysautonomia: heart coherence education and stellate ganglion block (SGB).

Coherence results when all body systems work together in harmony and reflects in relatively high heart rate variability (HRV) patterns. Graphically, the pattern of time between heart beats appears smooth and indicates interbeat flexibility. Techniques to attain this state include shifting attention to the heart and imagining breath entering and leaving it and evoking positive emotions and thoughts to strengthen coherence. The idea is to improve emotional self regulation and many have experienced positive effects of this including pilots and police. Coherence education improves hypertension, PTSD and congestive heart failure.

A procedure called SGB interrupts neural communication from the heart to the brain. The net effect displays as reduced sympathetic neural responses and improved blood flow to the brain and other peripherals. Recent research shows that SGB improves anxiety and other PTSD symptoms, however, it effects positive change also in pain perception, ventricular arrhythmias, and hot flashes.

SGB and coherence treatment approaches work because they reset the cardiac autonomic nervous system and nudge it toward a state of sympathovagal balance. Researchers have found that other reset methods improve health too. These include resets in bright light exposure, diet and feeding times, and sleep rhythms. Many who have used these methods report improved sleep and mood, less pain, and more energy.

15. Conclusion

As human creatures, like all other life forms, we operate best in rhythmic harmony with the earth, itself a planet in synchrony within a vast universe. We detect and respond to patterns of energy, such as light, in the environments outside our bodies. Because we function in a rhythmic manner, others can sync with our rhythms and we can sync with the rhythms of others who express rhythmic behavior. Our ability to create and respond to music, with its perceptible sound wave patterns, is an example of this. We're not alone in our ability to emit rhythmic signals and respond to them. Humans share this propensity with other living creatures. In a sense, our connectedness through bioenergetic rhythms is a natural and unavoidable part of who we are and how we operate. Entrainment via our circadian biorhythms to the daily rhythm of the earth rotating around the sun, for instance, is key to our survival. Internal entrainment across organs, which the brain-based suprachiasmatic nucleus directs, is key to health. Organs, in turn, with their own clock-like mechanisms, orchestrate activity across different tissue types that make up each organ. Such coordination is critical for the efficient and effective completion of life tasks. In this way, tasks such as growth, begin together and end together.

There are occasions, however, when synchronization with the world outside our bodies does not occur. We may purposely disrupt entrainment to accomplish a goal such as working the night shift. When healthy, we can recover relatively quickly from the effects of dysynchrony and return to a state where our circadian entrains again with the 24 hour geophysical cycle. Loss of synchrony with the earth's rhythm occurs also when we become sick and this seems to happen unconsciously, as if our bodies have decided to detach from external rhythms without announcing it formally to our conscious selves. The resulting biorhythm shift indicates psychophysiological defense shift too. This can go two ways: we retreat too much or we engage too much.

The focus in this book is on the group that tends to use excessive retreat as their main defense style. Excessive retreat signals illness because it means that the body has shifted biorhythms and defense to increase repair time and reduce further threat. This model of body repair offers a helpful lens through which CFS can be understood. One of the purposes of this book is tho expand the conversation about and thus understanding of CFS. The first major point is that CFS is a response to chronic distress, whether internal, external or both and displays characteristics of hibernation and biorhythm shift.

Relatively new discoveries about CFS allow us to reconsider key symptoms associated with it. An important alternative view is that many CFS symptoms link back to damaged cardiomyocytes. Since heart damage occurs, the odds of brain damage are high too.[1,2] Neuroinflammation and thus neural damage is a likely sequel which explains cognitive and mood problems. Certainly, fatigue, post-exertional malaise, and depression emanate from cardiovascular damage. One of the main ways cardiovascular disruption shows up is through dysautonomia.[3] Together with endothelial dysfunction (ED), they are precursors to and create the conditions for symptoms such as orthostatic intolerance, Raynaud's, and cognitive problems. This happens because ED and dysautonomia alter blood flow and distribution to the brain, hands and feet. One effect observed among those with CFS is brain hypoperfusion[4] (reduced blood distribution), which disrupts both resource supply and waste removal from brain tissue.

Another relatively new view of CFS concerns the cause of body-wide pain. Here it is localized to slow- and fast-twitch muscles. They behave as though they are operating in hypoxic conditions. This in turn nudges them toward using a different biofuel which eventually causes mitochondrial disturbance and pain.[5] Relatively high lactate levels among those with CFS offers some evidence of this biofuel switch.[6]

Here, the explanation for poor sleep experienced by those with CFS is expanded. Heightened sympathetic activity accounts partially for sleep problems,[7] however, the more important point is that such dysautonomia confirms that the autonomic nervous system has broken down to some extent.

The same system regulates body temperature control and disruption here explains poor sleep too since the ability to lower temperature is required to enter NREM sleep.[8] In addition, the ability to reduce or shut off body defenses against extreme heat and cold is required to enter REM.[9] Difficulties with body temperature control during sleep show up as irregularities in transitions from NREM to REM and vice versa. These types of sleep anomalies are observed among those with CFS.[10]

Autoimmunity is yet another symptom of CFS and a few different types of it display.[11] Regarding the cardiovascular system, autoimmunity is evident in immune cell attacks on adrenergic and muscarinic receptors and on mitochondrial lipids like cardiolipin. The latter, increases the odds of developing antiphospholipid syndrome. Some researchers believe that immune cells operate like an extension of the nervous system.[12] From this perspective, it is possible that autoimmune activity is an attempt by the nervous system to shut down cellular responses to substances such as adrenaline. If we consider existence of an internal defense cascade, apart from cellular biochemical pathways, then we can speculate that it works in the following way. First, the autonomic nervous system tries to exert control by altering neurotransmitter (e.g., noradrenaline) levels but if this does not work then cardiovascular defense kicks in via changes in blood pressure, distribution and flow. If the threat persists, then immune cells activate and engage resistance or fight. This is followed by tolerance to avoid further collateral damage. Upon a return to fighting, the immune cells now target more signs of pathogenic infection or toxin sources. This intensified attack may then play out as autoimmunity and could be the body's last-ditch effort to rid itself of unwanted toxins or other hazards.

It is worth noting that approaches to rectifying biological dysynchrony are also ways to restore autonomic and enhance voluntary neural control. One reason we experience sleep problems, for instance, is because a behavior (sleep) that is usually under autonomic or unconscious control enters the realm of voluntary or conscious control. The gist of Guy Meadow's sleep improvement method, for example, is to push control of sleep back into the autonomic realm.[13] He believes that one way to do this is to make the brain feel safe via acceptance and commitment therapy. When it's hard to fall asleep due to intrusive thoughts, for instance, Meadows suggests that we tell ourselves that the worrying thoughts are OK, even welcomed because they are doing their job which is to protect us. What we are learning, through studies of coherence and stellate ganglion block, among other research, is that it's even more important to make the heart feel safe. Improving emotional self-regulation helps to accomplish this,[14] which brings us to another part of addressing dysautonomia. The other part is to bring emotional responses that seem to occur automatically, like an anger outburst, back under voluntary control. If you think about it, this is an incredibly powerful way to give ourselves agency over health and wellbeing. The idea is to control ourselves so that we can control our own world experiences; acknowledging at the same time that many challenging life conditions are beyond our control. The research tells us though that self management is indeed possible and beneficial. Further, increased understanding of our biorhythms and defense styles gives us the tools we need to maximize health.

Long ago, our ancestors tuned into the rhythms of the world that surrounded them. We see signs of this awareness in many ancient symbols and constructions from the stone and tunnel arrangements of the prehistoric Newgrange passage tomb to the Mayan step pyramids. Being human, we leveraged this knowledge to navigate the planet and gather resources. The inward manifestation of such navigation became medicine, an attempt to understand and systematize methods to advance our health and defend against threats to it. We are still exploring this internal terrain. What is becoming evident, however, is that the more we understand our biorhythms and psychophysiological defense strategies, and the more we apply this knowledge to health and wellbeing, the more we remain in harmony with ourselves, our communities, our planet and the vast universe to which we all belong.

Bibliography

1. The Nature of Threat and Defense

1. Roelofs, Karin. Freeze for action: neurobiological mechanisms in animal and human freezing Philosophical Transactions of the Royal Society of London, Series Biological Sciences 2017; Apr 19;372(1718):20160206. https://doi: 10.1098/rstb.2016.0206.

2. Livermore, James A, Klaassen, Felix H, Bramson, Bob, et al. Approach-avoidance decisions under threat: The role of autonomic psychophysiological states. Frontiers in Neuroscience 2021; Mar 31;15:621517. https://doi: 10.3389/fnins.2021.621517. eCollection 2021.

3. Kozlowska, Kasia, Walker Peter, McLean Loyola, Carrive Pascal. Fear and the defense cascade: Clinical implications and management. Harvard Review of Psychiatry Jul-Aug 2015;23(4):263-87. https://doi: 10.1097/HRP.0000000000000065.

4. Drew Kelly L, Buck C Loren, Barnes Brian M, Christian Sherri L, Rasley Brian T, Harris Michael B. Central nervous system regulation of mammalian hibernation: implications for metabolic suppression and ischemia tolerance. Journal of Neurochemistry 2007 Sep;102(6):1713-1726. https://doi: 10.1111/j.1471-4159.2007.04675.x. Epub 2007 Jun 6.

5. Carey Hannah V, Andrews Matthew T, Martin Sandra L. Mammalian hibernation: cellular and molecular responses to depressed metabolism and low temperature. Physiological

Reviews 2003 83, 1153–1181. https://doi: 10.1152/physrev.00008.2003.

6. Thomas Ruf, Geiser Fritz. Daily torpor and hibernation in birds and mammals. Biological Reviews of the Cambridge Philosophical Society 2015 Aug;90(3):891-926. https://doi: 10.1111/brv.12137. Epub 2014 Aug 15.

7. Dausmann Kathrin H, Glos Julian, Ganzhorn Jorg U, Heldmaier Gerhard. Hibernation in the tropics: lessons from a primate. Journal of Comparative Physiology 2005 Apr;175(3):147-55. https://doi: 10.1007/s00360-004-0470-0. Epub 2005 Jan 29.

8. Nowack Julia, Mzilikazi Nomakwezi, Dausmann Kathrin H. Torpor on demand: heterothermy in the non-lemur primate Galago moholi PLoS One 2010; 5(5): e10797. https://doi: 10.1371/journal.pone.0010797.

9. Kortner Gerhard, Geiser Fritz, The temporal organization of daily torpor and hibernation: circadian and circannual rhythms. Chronobiology International 2000 Mar;17(2):103-28. https://doi: 10.1081/cbi-100101036.

10. Giroud Sylvain, Chery Isabelle, Bertile Fabrice, et al. Lipidomics reveals seasonal shifts in a large-bodied hibernator, the brown bear. Frontiers in Physiology 2019 Apr 12;10:389. https://doi: 10.3389/fphys.2019.00389. eCollection 2019.

11. Tater Marc, Yin Chih-Ming. Slow aging during insect reproductive diapause: why butterflies, grasshoppers and flies are like worms. Experimental Gerontology 2001 Apr;36(4-6):723-38. https://doi: 10.1016/s0531-5565(00)00238-2.

12. Nelson Ralph A. Protein and fat metabolism in hibernating bears. Federation Proceedings 1980 Oct;39(12):2955-8. PMID: 6998737.

13. Gonzalez-Riano Carolina, León-Espinosa Gonzalo, Regalado-Reyes Mamen, García Antonia, DeFelipe Javier,

Barbas Coral. Metabolomic study of hibernating Syrian hamster brains: In search of neuroprotective agents. Journal of Proteome Research 2019 Mar 1;18(3):1175-1190. https://doi: 10.1021/acs.jproteome.8b00816. Epub 2019 Jan 22. PMID: 30623656.

14. Kloner Robert A. Stunned and hibernating myocardium: Where are we nearly 4 decades later? Journal of the American Heart Association 2020 Feb 4;9(3). https://doi: 10.1161/JAHA.119.015502. Epub 2020 Feb 4.

15. Cannon. Walter B. Bodily Changes in Pain, Hunger, Fear and Rage. New York, NY: D. Appleton and Company; 1925.

16. Hofer Myron A. Cardiac and respiratory function during sudden prolonged immobility in wild rodents. Psychosomatic Medicine 1970; 32:633- 47. https://doi: 10.1097/00006842-197011000-00008.

17. Matzinger Polly. The danger model: a renewed sense of self. Science 2002 Apr 12;296(5566)):301-5. https://doi: 10.1126/science.1071059.

18. Dhabhar Firdaus S, McEwen Bruce S. Acute stress enhances while chronic stress suppresses cell-mediated immunity in vivo: a potential role for leukocyte trafficking. Brain Behavior and Immunity 1997 Dec; 11(4):286-306. https://doi: 10.1006/brbi.1997.0508.

19. Holmes Thomas H, Rahe Richard H, The Social Readjustment Rating Scale. Journal of Psychosomatic Research 1967;11(2):213-218. https://doi: 10.1016/0022-3999(67)90010-4.

20. Picard Martin, McEwen Bruce S. Psychological stress and mitochondria: A conceptual framework. Psychosomatic Medicine Feb/Mar 2018;80(2):126-140. https://doi: 10.1097/PSY.0000000000000544.

21. Dhabhar Firdaus S. The short-term stress response – mother nature's mechanism for enhancing protection and performance under conditions of threat, challenge, and opportunity. Frontiers in Neuroendocrinology 2018 Apr;49:175-192. https://doi: 10.1016/j.yfrne.2018.03.004. Epub 2018 Mar 26.

22. Selye, Hans. A syndrome produced by diverse noxious agents. 1936. The Journal of Neuropsychiatry and Clinical Neurosciences 1998 Spring;10(2):230-1. https://doi: 10.1176/jnp.10.2.230a.

23. Selye, Hans. Stress and the general adaptation syndrome. British Medical Journal 1950 Jun 17; 1(4667): 1383–1392. https://doi:10.1136/bmj.1.4667.1383.

24. Klaassen, Felix H, Held Leslie, Figner Bernd, et al. Defensive freezing and its relation to approach–avoidance decision-making under threat. Scientific Reports 2021 Jun 8;11(1):12030. https://doi: 10.1038/s41598-021-90968-z.

2. Biorhythms

1. Buijs Ruud M, van Eden Corbert G, Goncharuk Valerie D, Kalsbeek Andries. The biological clock tunes the organs of the body: timing by hormones and the autonomic nervous system. The Journal of Endocrinology 2003 Apr; 177(1):17-26. htttps://doi: 10.1677/joe.0.1770017.

2. Poggiogalle Eleonora, Humaira Jamshed, Peterson Courtney M. Circadian regulation of glucose, lipid, and energy metabolism in humans. Metabolism 2018 Jul;84:11-27. https://doi: 10.1016/j.metabol.2017.11.017. Epub 2018 Jan 9.

3. Labrecque Nathalie, Cermakian Nicolas. Circadian clocks in the immune system. Journal of Biological Rhythms 2015 Aug;30(4):277-90. https://doi: 10.1177/0748730415577723. Epub 2015 Apr 20.

4. Born Jan, Lange Tanja, Hansen Kirsten S, Molle Matthias, Fehm Horst-Lorenz. Effects of sleep and circadian rhythm on human circulating immune cells. Journal of Immunology 1997 May 1;158(9):4454-64.

5. Zhang Lilei, Jain Mukesh K. Circadian regulation of cardiac metabolism. The Journal of Clinical Investigation 2021 Aug 2;131(15):e148276. https://doi: 10.1172/JCI148276.

6. Begemann Kimberly, Neumann Anne-Marie, Oster Henrik. Regulation and function of extra-SCN circadian oscillators in the brain. Acta Physiologica (Oxford, England) 2020 May;229(1):e13446. https://doi: 10.1111/apha.13446. Epub 2020 Feb 6.

7. Maes Michael, Stevens Wim, Scharpe Simon, et al. Seasonal variation in peripheral blood leukocyte subsets and in serum interleukin-6, and soluble interleukin 2 and -6 receptor concentrations in normal volunteers. Experientia 1994;50:821–829. https://doi: 10.1007/BF01956463.

8. Lewis Jo E, Ebling Francis J. Tanycytes as regulators of seasonal cycles in neuroendocrine function. Frontiers in Neurology 2017;8:79. https://doi: 10.3389/fneur.2017.00079. eCollection 2017.

9. Foster Russell G, Roenneberg Till. Human responses to the geophysical daily, annual and lunar cycles. Current Biology 2008 Sep 9;18(17):R784-R794. https://doi: 10.1016/j.cub.2008.07.003.

10. Hastings Michael H, Reddy Akhilesh B, Maywood Elizabeth S. A clockwork web: Circadian timing in brain and periphery, in health and disease. Nature Reviews. Neuroscience 2003 Aug;4(8):649-61. https://doi: 10.1038/nrn1177.

11. Stehle Jorge H, Saade Anastasia, Rawashdeh Oliver, et al. A survey of molecular details in the human pineal gland in the light of phylogeny, structure, function and chronobiological

diseases. Journal of Pineal Research 2011 Aug;51(1):17-43. htpps://doi: 10.1111/j.1600-079X.2011.00856.x. Epub 2011 Apr 26.

12. Pell Jill P, Cobbe Stuart M. Seasonal variations in coronary heart disease. Monthly Journal of the Association of Physicians 1999 Dec;92(12):689-96. https://doi: 10.1093/qjmed/92.12.689.

13. Erren Thomas C, Reiter Russel J. Defining chronodisruption. Journal of Pineal Research 2009 Apr;46(3):245-7. https://doi: 10.1111/j.1600-079X.2009.00665.x. Epub 2009 Feb 9.

14. Zhang Luoying, Ptacek Louis J, Fu Ying-Hui. Diversity of human clock genotypes and consequences. Progress in Molecular Biology and Translational Science 2013;119:51-81. https://doi: 10.1016/B978-0-12-396971-2.00003-8.

15. Agorastos Agorastos, Olff Miranda. Traumatic stress and the circadian system: neurobiology, timing and treatment of posttraumatic chronodisruption. European Journal of Psychotraumatology 2020 Nov 27;11(1):1833644. doi: 10.1080/20008198.2020.1833644.

16. Gillette Martha U, Tischkau Shelley A. Suprachiasmatic nucleus: the brain's circadian clock. Recent Progress in Hormone Research 1999;54:33-58.

17. Hardin, Paul E., Hall, Jeffrey C., and Rosbash, Michael. Feedback of the Drosophila period gene product on circadian cycling of its messenger RNA levels. Nature 1990 Feb 8;343(6258):536-40. https://doi: 10.1038/343536a0.

18. Gekakis, Nicholas, Saez, Lino, Delahaye-Brown, Anne-Marie, et al. Isolation of timeless by PER protein interaction: defective interaction between timeless protein and long-period mutant PERL. Science 1995 Nov 3;270(5237):811-5. https://doi: 10.1126/science.270.5237.811.

19. Adamovich Yaarit, Ladeuix Benjamin, Golik Marina, Koeners Maaarten P, Asher Gad. Rhythmic Oxygen Levels Reset Circadian Clocks through HIF1α. Cell Metabolism 2017 Jan 10;25(1):93-101. https://doi: 10.1016/j.cmet.2016.09.014. Epub 2016 Oct 20.

20. Milev Nikolay B, Rhee Sue-Goo, Reddy Akhilesh B. Cellular timekeeping: It's redox o'clock. Cold Spring Harbor Perspectives in Biology 2018 May 1;10(5):a027698. Https://doi: 10.1101/cshperspect.a027698.

21. Guan Junwen, Ding Yuanlin, Liu Yanyu, Li Yonghong, Wang Zhengrong Circadian effects on outcome following surgery for intracerebral hemorrhage in humans? Brain Research 2009 Mar 3;1258:78-85. https://doi: 10.1016/j.brainres.2008.11.106. Epub 2008 Dec 31.

22. Guan Junwen, You Chaoy, Liu Yanyu, Zhang Rong, Wang Zhengrong. Characteristics of infradian and circadian rhythms in the persistent vegetative state. The Journal of International Medical Research 2011;39(6):2281-7. https://doi: 10.1177/147323001103900625.

23. Longo Valter D, Panda Satchidananda. Fasting, circadian rhythms, and time-restricted feeding in healthy lifespan. Cell Metabolism 2016 Jun 14;23(6):1048-1059. https://doi: 10.1016/j.cmet.2016.06.001.

24. Muradyan Arpine, Macheiner Tanja, Mardiyan Marine, Sekoyan Eduard, Sargsyan Karine. The evaluation of biomarkers of physical activity on stress resistance and wellness. Applied Psychophysiology and Biofeedback 2022 Jun;47(2):121-129. https://doi: 10.1007/s10484-022-09538-2. Epub 2022 Mar 16.

25. Lewy Alfred J, Emens Jonathan, Jackman Angela, Yuhas Krista. Circadian uses of melatonin in humans. Chronobiology International 2006;23(1-2):403-12. https://doi: 10.1080/07420520500545862.

26. Chodron Pema. The Wisdom of No Escape and the Path of Loving Kindness. Boulder, CO: Shambhala Inc., 1991.

27. Besedovsky Luciana, Lange Tanja, Haack Monika. The sleep-immune crosstalk in health and disease. Physiological Reviews 2019 Jul 1;99(3):1325-1380. https://doi: 10.1152/physrev.00010.2018.

28. Cambras Trinitat, Castro-Marrero Jesus, Zaragoza Maria C, Diez-Noguera Antoni, Alegre Jose. Circadian rhythm abnormalities and autonomic dysfunction in patients with Chronic Fatigue Syndrome/Myalgic Encephalomyelitis. PLoS One 2018 Jun 6;13(6):e0198106. https://doi: 10.1371/journal.pone.0198106. eCollection 2018.

29. Jackson Melinda L, Bruck Dorothy. Sleep abnormalities in chronic fatigue syndrome/myalgic encephalomyelitis: A review. Journal of Clinical Sleep Medicine 2012 Dec 15;8(6):719-28. Https://doi: 10.5664/jcsm.2276.

30. Leng Yue, Musiek Erik S, Hu Kun, Cappuccio Francesco P, Yaffe Kristine. Association between circadian rhythms and neurodegenerative diseases. The Lancet. Neurology 2019 Mar;18(3):307-318. https://doi: 10.1016/S1474-4422(18)30461-7. Epub 2019 Feb 12.

31. Odintsova Tetiana A, Kopchak Oksana O. Sleep disorders in relapsing-remitting multiple sclerosis patients. Wiadomosci Lekarskie 2021;74(2):257-262. https://doi:10.36740/WLek202102115.

32. Truong Kimberly K, Lam Michael T, Grandner Michael A, Sassoon Catherine S, Malhotra Atul. Timing matters: Circadian rhythm in sepsis, obstructive lung disease, obstructive sleep apnea, and cancer. Annals of the American Thoracic Society 2016 Jul;13(7):1144-54. https://doi: 10.1513/AnnalsATS.201602-125FR.

33. Bertisch Suzanne M, Pollock Benjamin D, Mittleman Murray A, et al. Insomnia with objective short sleep duration

and risk of incident cardiovascular disease and all-cause mortality: Sleep Heart Health Study. Sleep 2018 Jun 1;41(6):zsy047. https://doi: 10.1093/sleep/zsy047.

34. Foster Russell G. Sleep, circadian rhythms and health. Interface Focus 2020 Jun 6;10(3):20190098. doi: 10.1098/rsfs.2019.0098. Epub 2020 Apr 17.

35. Vandewalle Giles, Archer Simon N, Wuillaume Catherine, et al. Functional magnetic resonance imaging-assessed brain responses during an executive task depend on interaction of sleep homeostasis, circadian phase, and PER3 genotype. The Journal of Neuroscience 2009 Jun 24;29(25):7948-56. https://doi: 10.1523/JNEUROSCI.0229-09.2009.

36. Kettner Nicole M, Katchy Chinenye A, Fu Loning. Circadian gene variants in cancer. Annals of Medicine 2014 Jun;46(4):208-20. https://doi: 10.3109/07853890.2014.914808. Epub 2014 Jun 5.

37. Hansen Johnni. Night shift work and risk of breast cancer. Current Environmental Health Reports 2017 Sep;4(3):325-339. https://doi: 10.1007/s40572-017-0155-y. 4, 325–339.

38. Papantoniou Kyriaki, Castano-Vinyals Gemma, Espinosa Ana, et al. Shift work and colorectal cancer risk in the MCC-Spain case-control study. Scandinavian Journal of Work, Environment, and Health 2017 May 1;43(3):250-259. https://doi: 10.5271/sjweh.3626. Epub 2017 Mar 2.

39. Conlon Michael, Lightfoot Nancy, Kreiger Nancy. Rotating shift work and risk of prostate cancer. Epidemiology 2007 Jan;18(1):182-3. https://doi: 10.1097/01.ede.0000249519.33978.31.

40. Liu Wen, Zhou Zhonghan, Dong Dahai, Sun Lijang, Zhang Guiming. Sex differences in the association between night shift work and the risk of cancers: A meta-analysis of 57 articles. Disease Markers. 2018 Nov 26;2018:7925219. https://doi: 10.1155/2018/7925219. eCollection 2018.

41. Lange Tanja, Perras Boris, Fehm Horst L, Born Jan. Sleep enhances the human antibody response to hepatitis A vaccination. Psychosomatic Medicine 2003 Sep-Oct;65(5):831-5. https://doi: 10.1097/01.psy.0000091382.61178.f1.

42. Spiegel Karine, Sheridan John F, Van Cauter Eve. Effect of sleep deprivation on response to immunization. Journal of the American Medical Association 2002 Sep 25;288(12):1471-2. https://doi: 10.1001/jama.288.12.1471-a.

43. Erren Thomas C, Koch Melissa S, Groß J Valeri, et al. Chronomedicine: an old concept's fledging? A selective literature search. Neuro Endocrinology Letters 2012;33(4):357-60. PMID: 22936255.

44. Otsuka Kuniaki, Cornélissen Germaine, Halberg Franz. Circadian rhythms and clinical chronobiology. Biomedicine and Pharmacotherapy 2001;55 Suppl 1:7s-18s. https://doi: 10.1016/s0753-3322(01)90000-9.

45. Coudert Bruno, Focan Christian, Genet Dominique, et al. A randomized multicenter study of optimal circadian time of vinorelbine combined with chronomodulated 5-fluorouracil in pretreated metastatic breast cancer patients: EORTC trial 05971. Chronobiology International 2008 Sep;25(5):680-96. https://doi: 10.1080/07420520802384036.

46. Asao Takayuki, Sakurai Hideyuki, Harashima Kouichi, et al. The synchronization of chemotherapy to circadian rhythms and irradiation in pre-operative chemoradiation therapy with hyperthermia for local advanced rectal cancer. International Journal of Hyperthermia 2006 Aug;22(5):399-406. https://doi: 10.1080/02656730600799873.

47. Paudel Keshav R, Jha Saurav K, Allam Venkata S, et al. Recent advances in chronotherapy targeting respiratory diseases. Pharmaceutics 2021 Nov 25;13(12):2008. https://doi: 10.3390/pharmaceutics13122008.

48. Beam William R, Weiner Douglas E, Martin Richard J. Timing of prednisone and alterations of airways inflammation in nocturnal asthma . The American Review of Respiratory Disease 1992 Dec;146(6):1524-30. https://doi: 10.1164/ajrccm/146.6.1524.

49. Hermida Ramon C, Crespo Juan J, Domínguez-Sardiña Manuel, et al. Bedtime hypertension treatment improves cardiovascular risk reduction: the Hygia Chronotherapy Trial. European Heart Journal 2020 Dec 21;41(48):4565-4576. https://doi: 10.1093/eurheartj/ehz754.

3. Life Tasks

1. Verma Nagendra, Franchitto Matteo, Zonfrilli Azzurra, Cialfi Samantha, Palermo Rocco, Talora Claudia. DNA damage stress: Cui prodest? International Journal of Molecular Science 2019 Mar 1;20(5):1073. https://doi: 10.3390/ijms20051073.

2. Strzyz Paulina. Signalling to cell cycle arrest. Nature Reviews Molecular Cell Biology 2016 Sep;17(9):536. https://doi: 10.1038/nrm.2016.108. Epub 2016 Aug 10.

3. Aranda-Anzaldo Armando. The post-mitotic state in neurons correlates with a stable nuclear higher-order structure. Communicative and Integrative Biology 2012 Mar 1;5(2):134-9. https://doi: 10.4161/cib.18761.

4. Laflamme Michael, Murray Charles E. Heart regeneration. Nature 2011 May 19;473(7347):326-35. https://doi: 10.1038/nature10147.

5. Siddiqi Sailay, Sussman Mark A.The heart: Mostly postmitotic or mostly premitotic? Myocyte cell cycle, senescence and quiescence. The Canadian Journal of Cardiology 2014 Nov;30(11):1270-8. https://doi: 10.1016/j.cjca.2014.08.014. Epub 2014 Aug 23.

6. Li Yan, He Lingjuan, Huang Xiuzhen, et al. Genetic lineage tracing of non-myocyte population by dual recombinases. Circulation 2018 Aug 21;138(8):793-805. https://doi: 10.1161/CIRCULATIONAHA.118.034250.

7. Graham Evan, Bergmann Olaf. Dating the heart: Exploring cardiomyocyte renewal in humans. Physiology (Bethesda) 2017 Jan;32(1):33-41. https://doi: 10.1152/physiol.00015.2016.

8. Von Bernhardi Rommy, Bernhardi Laura E, Eugenín Jaime. What is neural plasticity? Advances in Experimental Medicine and Biology 2017;1015:1-15. https://doi: 10.1007/978-3-319-62817-2_1.

9. Bergmann Olaf, Spalding Kirsty L, Frisen Jonas. Adult neurogenesis in humans. Cold Spring Harbor Perspectives in Biology 2015 Jul 1;7(7):a018994. https://doi: 10.1101/cshperspect.a018994.

10. Kumar Ashutosh, Pareek Vikas, Faiq Muneeb S, Ghosh Sanjib K, Kumari Chiman. Adult neurogenesis in humans: A review of basic concepts, history, current research, and clinical implications. Innovations in Clinical Neuroscience 2019 May 1;16(5-6):30-37.

11. Hulbert AJ, Else Paul L. Membranes and the setting of energy demand. The Journal of Experimental Biology 2005 May;208(Pt 9):1593-9. htps://doi: 10.1242/jeb.01482.

12. Panda Satchidananda. Circadian physiology of metabolism. Science 2016 Nov 25;354(6315):1008-1015. https://doi: 10.1126/science.aah4967.

13. Hatanaka Fumiyuki, Takumi Toru. CHRONO integrates behavioral stress and epigenetic control of metabolism. Annals of Medicine 2017 Jun;49(4):352-356. https://doi: 10.1080/07853890.2016.1276301. Epub 2017 Jan 19.

14. Partch Carrie L. Orchestration of circadian timing by macromolecular assemblies. Journal of Molecular Biology

2020 May 29;432(12):3426-3448. https://doi: 10.1016/j.jmb.2019.12.046. Epub 2020 Jan 13.

15. Sinturel Flore, Petrenko Volodymyr, Dibner Charna. Circadian clocks make metabolism run. Journal of Molecular Biology 2020 May 29;432(12):3680-3699. doi: 10.1016/j.jmb.2020.01.018. Epub 2020 Jan 26.

16. Milev Nikolay B, Rhee Sue-Goo, Reddy Akhilesh B. Cellular timekeeping: It's redox o'clock. Cold Spring Harbor Perspectives in Biology 2018 May 1;10(5):a027698. https://doi: 10.1101/cshperspect.a027698.

17. Morris Andrew R, Stanton Daniel L, Roman Destino, Liu Andrew C. Systems level understanding of circadian integration with cell physiology. Journal of Molecular Biology 2020 May 29;432(12):3547-3564. https://doi: 10.1016/j.jmb.2020.02.002. Epub 2020 Feb 13.

18. Tu Benjamin P, Kudlicki Andrzej, Rowicka Maga, McKnight Steven L. Logic of the yeast metabolic cycle: temporal compartmentalization of cellular processes. Science 2005 Nov 18;310(5751):1152-8. https://doi: 10.1126/science.1120499. Epub 2005 Oct 27.

19. Kondo Takao, Mori Tetsuya, Lebedeva Natalia V, Aoki Setsuyuki, Ishiura Masahiro, Golden Susan S. Circadian rhythms in rapidly dividing cyanobacteria. Science 1997 Jan 10;275(5297):224-7. https://doi: 10.1126/science.275.5297.224.

20. Nagoshi Emi, Saini Camille, Bauer Christoph, Laroche Thierry, Naef Felix, Schibler Ueli. Circadian gene expression in individual fibroblasts: cell-autonomous and self-sustained oscillators pass time to daughter cells. Cell 2004 Nov 24;119(5):693-705. https://doi: 10.1016/j.cell.2004.11.015.

21. Tu Benjamin P, McKnight Steven L. The yeast metabolic cycle: insights into the life of a eukaryotic cell. Cold Spring Harbor Symposia on Quantitative Biology 2007;72:339-43. https://doi: 10.1101/sqb.2007.72.019.

22. Ciccia Alberto, Elledge Stephen J. The DNA damage response: making it safe to play with knives. Molecular Cell 2010 Oct 22;40(2):179-204. https://doi: 10.1016/j.molcel.2010.09.019.

23. Gawriluk Thomas R, Simkin Jennifer, Hacker Corin K. Complex tissue regeneration in mammals is associated with reduced inflammatory cytokines and an influx of T cells. Frontiers in Immunology 2020 Aug 7;11:1695. https://doi: 10.3389/fimmu.2020.01695. eCollection 2020.

24. Chatterjee Somik, Ma Ke. Circadian clock regulation of skeletal muscle growth and repair. F1000Res 2016 Jun 30;5:1549. https://doi: 10.12688/f1000research.9076.1. eCollection 2016.

25. Psarras Stelios, Beis Dimitris, Nikouli Sofia, Tsikitis Mary, Capetanaki Yassemi. Three in a Box: Understanding Cardiomyocyte, Fibroblast, and Innate Immune Cell Interactions to Orchestrate Cardiac Repair Processes. Frontiers in Cardiovascular Medicine 2019 Apr 2;6:32. https://doi: 10.3389/fcvm.2019.00032. eCollection 2019.

26. Armour J. Andrew, Ardell Jeffrey L. Basic and Clinical Neurocardiology. New York, NY: Oxford University Press; 2004.

27. Cao Jingli, Poss Kenneth D. The epicardium as a hub for heart regeneration. Nature Reviews. Cardiology 2018 Oct;15(10):631-647. https://doi: 10.1038/s41569-018-0046-4.

28. Lombardi Duccio, Lasagni Laura. Cell-cycle alterations in post-mitotic cells and cell death by mitotic catastrophe, In: Cell Biology New Insights (Editor, Stevo Najman). Rijeka, Croatia: InTech; 2016:59-90.

29. Guan Junwen, You Chaoy, Liu Yanyu, Zhang Rong, Wang Zhengrong. Characteristics of infradian and circadian rhythms in the persistent vegetative state. The Journal of

International Medical Research 2011;39(6):2281-7. https://doi: 10.1177/147323001103900625.

30. Carey Hannah, Andrews Matthew, Martin Sandra. Mammalian hibernation: cellular and molecular responses to depressed metabolism and low temperature. Physiological Reviews 2003 Oct;83(4):1153-81. doi: 10.1152/physrev.00008.2003.

31. Storey Kenneth B, Storey Janet M. Metabolic regulation and gene expression during aestivation. Progress in Molecular and Subcellular Biology 2010;49:25-45. https://doi: 10.1007/978-3-642-02421-4_2.

4. Hibernation

1. Gonzalez-Bernado Enrique, Russo Luca F, Valderrabano Esther, Fernandez Angel, Penteriani Vincenzo. Denning in brown bears. Ecology and Evolution 2020 May 25;10(13):6844-6862. https://doi: 10.1002/ece3.6372. eCollection 2020 Jul.

2. Harding Edward C, Franks Nicholas P, Wisden William. The temperature dependence of sleep. Frontiers in Neuroscience 2019 Apr 24;13:336. https://doi: 10.3389/fnins.2019.00336.

3. Carey Hannah, Andrews Matthew, Martin Sandra. Mammalian hibernation: cellular and molecular responses to depressed metabolism and low temperature. Physiological Reviews 2003 Oct;83(4):1153-81. doi: 10.1152/physrev.00008.2003.

4. Storey Kenneth B, Storey Janet M. Metabolic regulation and gene expression during aestivation. Progress in Molecular and Subcellular Biology 2010;49:25-45. https://doi: 10.1007/978-3-642-02421-4_2.

5. Mayo Clinic Staff. Basal Body temperature for natural family planning. www. mayoclinic.org, accessed 07/17/2022.

6. Frare Carla, Williams Cory T, Drew Kelly L. Thermoregulation in hibernating mammals: The role of the "thyroid hormones system." Molecular and Cellular Endocrinology 2021 Jan 1;519:111054. https://doi: 10.1016/j.mce.2020.111054. Epub 2020 Oct 7.

7. Epperson L Elaine, Karimpour-Fard Anis, Hunter Lawrence E, Martin Sandra L. Metabolic cycles in a circannual hibernator. Physiological Genomics 2011 Jul 14;43(13):799-807. https://doi: 10.1152/physiolgenomics.00028.2011. Epub 2011 May 3.

8. Soo Elizabeth, Welch Anthony, Marsh Christopher, McKay Dianne B. Molecular strategies used by hibernators: Potential therapeutic directions for ischemia reperfusion injury and preservation of human donor organs. Transplantation Reviews (Orlando) 2020 Jan;34(1):100514. https://doi: 10.1016/j.trre.2019.100514. Epub 2019 Oct 17.

9. Storey Kenneth B, Storey Jane M. Metabolic rate depression in animals: transcriptional and translational controls. Biological Reviews of the Cambridge Philosophical Society 2004 Feb;79(1):207-33. https://doi: 10.1017/s1464793103006195.

10. Giroud Sylvain, Habold Caroline, Nespolo Roberto F, et al. The torpid state: Recent advances in metabolic adaptations and protective mechanisms. Frontiers in Physiology 2021 Jan 20;11:623665. https://doi: 10.3389/fphys.2020.623665. eCollection 2020.

11. Dark John. Annual lipid cycles in hibernators: integration of physiology and behavior. Annual Review of Nutrition 2005;25:469-97. https://doi: 10.1146/annurev.nutr.25.050304.092514.

12. Staples James F. Metabolic flexibility: Hibernation, torpor, and estivation. Comprehensive Physiology 2016 Mar 15;6(2):737-71. https://doi: 10.1002/cphy.c140064.

13. Chanon Stephanie, Chazarin Blandine, Toubhans Benoit, et al. Proteolysis inhibition by hibernating bear serum leads to increased protein content in human muscle cells. Scientific Reports 2018 Apr 3;8(1):5525. https://doi: 10.1038/s41598-018-23891-5.

14. Welinder Karen G, Hansen Rasmus, Overgaard Michael T, et al. Biochemical foundations of health and energy conservation in hibernating free-ranging subadult brown bear Ursus Arctos. The Journal of Biological Chemistry 2016 Oct 21;291(43):22509-22523. https://doi: 10.1074/jbc.M116.742916. Epub 2016 Sep 8.

15. Morin Pier Jr, Storey Kenneth B. Mammalian hibernation: differential gene expression and novel application of epigenetic controls. The International Journal of Developmental Biology 2009;53(2-3):433-42. https://doi: 10.1387/ijdb.082643pm.

16. Tsukamoto Daisuke, Ito Michihiko, Takamatsu Nobuhiko. Epigenetic regulation of hibernation-associated HP-20 and HP-27 gene transcription in chipmunk liver. Biochemical and Biophysical Research Communications 2018 Jan 8;495(2):1758-1765. https://doi: 10.1016/j.bbrc.2017.12.052. Epub 2017 Dec 9.

17. Landes Julie, Pavard Samuel, Pierre-Yves Henry, Terrien Jeremy. Flexibility Is Costly: Hidden Physiological Damage From Seasonal Phenotypic Transitions in Heterothermic Species. Frontiers in Physiology 2020 Aug 12;11:985. https://doi: 10.3389/fphys.2020.00985. eCollection 2020.

18. Mergenthaler Philipp, Lindauer Ute, Dienel Gerald A, Meisel Andreas. Sugar for the brain: the role of glucose in physiological and pathological brain function. Trends in Neurosciences 2013 Oct;36(10):587-97. https://doi: 10.1016/j.tins.2013.07.001. Epub 2013 Aug 20.

19. Jiang Haibo, He C, Fong LG, Young SG. The fatty acids from LPL-mediated processing of triglycerides-rich

lipoproteins are taken up rapidly by cardiomyocytes. Journal of Lipid Research 2020 Jun;61(6):815. https://doi: 10.1194/jlr.ILR120000783. Epub 2020 Apr 2.

20. Rigano Kimberly S, Gehring Joelle L, Evans Hutzenbiler Brandon D, et al. Life in the fat lane: seasonal regulation of insulin sensitivity, food intake, and adipose biology in brown bears. Journal of Comparative Physiology B 2017 May;187(4):649-676. https://doi: 10.1007/s00360-016-1050-9. Epub 2016 Dec 16.

21. Heyde Isabel, Begemann Kimberly, Oster Henrik. Contributions of white and brown adipose tissues to the circadian regulation of energy metabolism. Endocrinology 2021 Mar 1;162(3):bqab009. https://doi: 10.1210/endocr/bqab009.

22. Ballinger Mallory A, Andrews Matthew T. Nature's fat-burning machine: brown adipose tissue in a hibernating mammal. The Journal of Experimental Biology 2018 Mar 7;221(Pt Suppl 1):jeb162586. https://doi: 10.1242/jeb.162586.

23. Martin Sandra L. Water balance: Abstaining from obtaining while retaining. Current Biology 2019 Oct 7;29(19):R925-R927. doi: 10.1016/j.cub.2019.08.038.

24. Rice Sarah A, Ten Have Gabriella AM, Reisz Julie A, et al. Nitrogen recycling buffers against ammonia toxicity from skeletal muscle breakdown in hibernating arctic ground squirrels. Nature Metabolism 2020 Dec;2(12):1459-1471. https://doi: 10.1038/s42255-020-00312-4. Epub 2020 Dec 7.

25. Schmidt Vanessa, Horvath Carla, Dong Hua, et al. SORLA is required for insulin-induced expansion of the adipocyte precursor pool in visceral fat. The Journal of Cellular Biology 2021 Dec 6;220(12):e202006058. doi: 10.1083/jcb.202006058. Epub 2021 Nov 15.

26. Hojlund Kurt. Metabolism and insulin signaling in common metabolic disorders and inherited insulin resistance. Danish Medical Journal 2014 Jul;61(7):B4890.

27. Sonsalla Michelle M, Love Santidra L, Hoh Laurana J, et al. Development of metabolic inflammation during pre-hibernation fattening in 13-lined ground squirrels (Ictidomys tridecemlineatus). Journal of Comparative Physiology B 2021 Sep;191(5):941-953. https://doi: 10.1007/s00360-021-01384-8. Epub 2021 Jun 24.

28. Doherty Alison H, Florant Gregory L, Donahue Seth W. Endocrine regulation of bone and energy metabolism in hibernating mammals. Integrative and Comparative Biology 2014 Sep;54(3):463-83. https://doi: 10.1093/icb/icu001. Epub 2014 Feb 19.

29. Wu Chong-Wen, Biggar Kyle K, Storey Kenneth B. Biochemical adaptations of mammalian hibernation: exploring squirrels as a perspective model for naturally induced reversible insulin resistance. Brazilian Journal of Medical and Biological Research 2013 Jan;46(1):1-13. https://doi: 10.1590/1414-431X20122388. Epub 2013 Jan 11.

30. Cotton Clarke J. Skeletal muscle mass and composition during mammalian hibernation. The Journal of Experimental Biology 2016 Jan;219(Pt 2):226-34. https://doi: 10.1242/jeb.125401.

31. Xu Ran, Andres-Mateos Eva, Mejias Rebeca, et al. Hibernating squirrel muscle activates the endurance exercise pathway despite prolonged immobilization. Experimental Neurology 2013 Sep;247:392-401. doi: 10.1016/j.expneurol.2013.01.005. Epub 2013 Jan 16.

32. Miyazaki Mitsunori, Shimozuru Michito, Tsubota Toshio. Skeletal muscles of hibernating black bears show minimal atrophy and phenotype shifting despite prolonged physical inactivity and starvation. PLoS One 2019 Apr 18;14(4):e0215489. https://doi: 10.1371/journal.pone.0215489. eCollection 2019.

33. Tessier Shannon N, Storey Kenneth B. Lessons from mammalian hibernators: Molecular insights into striated muscle plasticity and remodeling. Biomolecular Concepts 2016 May 1;7(2):69-92. doi: 10.1515/bmc-2015-0031.

34. Childers Christine L, Tessier Shannon N, Storey Kenneth B. The heart of a hibernator: EGFR and MAPK signaling in cardiac muscle during the hibernation of thirteen-lined ground squirrels, Ictidomys tridecemlineatus. PeerJ 2019 Sep 5;7:e7587. https://doi: 10.7717/peerj.7587. eCollection 2019.

35. Bouma Hjalmar R, Carey Hannah V, Kroese Frans GM. Hibernation: the immune system at rest? Journal of Leucocyte Biology 2010 Oct;88(4):619-24. https://doi: 10.1189/jlb.0310174. Epub 2010 Jun 2.

36. Sahdo Berolla, Evans Alina L, Arnemo Jon M, Fröbert Ole, Särndahl Eva, Blanc Stephan. Body temperature during hibernation is highly correlated with a decrease in circulating innate immune cells in the brown bear (Ursus arctos): a common feature among hibernators? International Journal of Medical Sciences 2013;10(5):508-14. https://doi: 10.7150/ijms.4476. Epub 2013 Mar 11.

37. Tessier Shannon N, Katzenback Barbara, Pifferi Fabien, Perret Martine, Storey Kenneth B. Cytokine and Antioxidant Regulation in the Intestine of the Gray Mouse Lemur (Microcebus murinus) During Torpor. Genomics Proteomics Bioinformatics 2015 Apr;13(2):127-35. https://doi: 10.1016/j.gpb.2015.03.005. Epub 2015 Jun 17.

38. Wei Yanhong, Zhang Jie, Yan Xia, et al. Remarkable protective effects of Nrf2-mediated antioxidant enzymes and tissue specificity in different skeletal muscles of Daurian ground squirrels over the torpor-arousal cycle. Frontiers in Physiology 2019 Nov 22;10:1449. https://doi: 10.3389/fphys.2019.01449. eCollection 2019.

39. Yin Quiyuan, Ge Hanxiao, Liao Chen-Chong, Liu Di, Zhang Shuyi, Pan Yi-Hsuan. Antioxidant defenses in the

brains of bats during hibernation. PLoS One 2016 Mar 24;11(3):e0152135. https://doi: 10.1371/journal.pone.0152135. eCollection 2016.

40. Benbrook Doris M, Long Ann. Integration of autophagy, proteasomal degradation, unfolded protein response and apoptosis. Experimental Oncology 2012 Oct;34(3):286-97.

41. Bagherniya Mohammad, Butler Alexandra E, Barreto George E, Sahebkar Amirhossein. The effect of fasting or calorie restriction on autophagy induction: A review of the literature. Ageing Research Reviews 2018 Nov;47:183-197. doi: 10.1016/j.arr.2018.08.004. Epub 2018 Aug 30.

42. Drew Kelly L. Rice Margaret E, Kuhn Thomas B, Smith Mark A. Neuroprotective adaptations in hibernation: Therapeutic implications for ischemia-reperfusion, traumatic brain injury, and neurodegenerative diseases. Free Radical Biology and Medicine 2001 Sep 1;31(5):563-73. https://doi: 10.1016/s0891-5849(01)00628-1.

43. Dugbartey George J, Bouma Hjalmar, Saha Manujendra N, Lobb Ian, Henning Robert H, Sener Alp. A hibernation-like state for transplantable organs: Is hydrogen sulfide therapy the future of organ preservation? Antioxidants and Redox Signaling 2018 Jun 1;28(16):1503-1515. https://doi: 10.1089/ars.2017.7127. Epub 2017 Aug 29.

44. Wu Dan, Gu Yijing, Zhu Deqiu. Cardioprotective effects of hydrogen sulfide in attenuating myocardial ischemia–reperfusion injury. Molecular Medicine Reports 2021 Dec;24(6):875. https://doi: 10.3892/mmr.2021.12515. Epub 2021 Nov 2.

45. Fu Zhifang, Liu Xinmin, Geng Bin, Fang Liping, Tang Chaoshu. Hydrogen sulfide protects rat lung from ischemia-reperfusion injury. Life Sciences 2008 Jun 6;82(23-24):1196-202. https://doi: 10.1016/j.lfs.2008.04.005. Epub 2008 May 15.

46. Wei Yanhong, Zhang Jie, Xu Shenhui, et al. Controllable oxidative stress and tissue specificity in major tissues during torpor-arousal cycle in hibernating Daurian ground squirrels. Open Biology 2018 Oct 10;8(10):180068. https://doi: 10.1098/rsob.180068.

47. Himelright Brendan M, Moore Jenna M, Gonzales Ramona L, et al. Sequential ovulation and fertility of polyoestrus in American black bears (Ursus Americanus). Conservation Physiology 2014 Nov 25;2(1):cou051. https://doi: 10.1093/conphys/cou051. eCollection 2014.

5. Sleep

1. Krueger James M, Frank Marcos G, Wisor Jonathan P, Roy Sandip. Sleep function: Toward elucidating an enigma. Sleep Medicine Reviews 2016 Aug;28:46-54. https://doi: 10.1016/j.smrv.2015.08.005. Epub 2015 Aug 28.

2. Reddy Oliver C, van der Werf Ysbrand D. The sleeping brain: Harnessing the power of the glymphatic system through lifestyle choices. Brain Sciences 2020 Nov 17;10(11):868. https://doi: 10.3390/brainsci10110868.

3. Benveniste Helene, Lee Hedok, Volkow Nora D. The glymphatic pathway: Waste removal from the CNS via cerebrospinal fluid transport. The Neuroscientist 2017 Oct;23(5):454-465. https://doi: 10.1177/1073858417691030. Epub 2017 Feb 2.

4. Besedovsky Luciana, Lange Tanja, Haack Monika.The sleep-immune crosstalk in health and disease. Physiological Reviews 2019 Jul 1;99(3):1325-1380. https://doi: 10.1152/physrev.00010.2018

5. Stehle Jorge H, Saade Anastasia, Rawashdeh Oliver, et al. A survey of molecular details in the human pineal gland in the light of phylogeny, structure, function and chronobiological diseases. Journal of Pineal Research 2011 Aug;51(1):17-43.

htpps://doi: 10.1111/j.1600-079X.2011.00856.x. Epub 2011 Apr 26.

6. Ben Simon Eti, Rossi Aubrey, Harvey Allison G, Walker Matthew P. Overanxious and underslept. Nature Human Behaviour 2020 Jan;4(1):100-110. https://doi: 10.1038/s41562-019-0754-8. Epub 2019 Nov 4.

7. Saconi Bruno, Polomano Rosemary C, Comptom Peggy C, McPhillips Miranda V, Kuna Samuel T, Sawyer Amy M. The influence of sleep disturbances and sleep disorders on pain outcomes among veterans: A systematic scoping review. Sleep Medicine Reviews 2021 Apr;56:101411. https://doi: 10.1016/j.smrv.2020.101411. Epub 2020 Nov 30.

8. Cao Junyu, Herman Alexander B, West Geoffrey B, Poe Gina, Savage Van M. Unraveling why we sleep: Quantitative analysis reveals abrupt transition from neural reorganization to repair in early development. Science Advances 2020 Sep 18;6(38):eaba0398. https://doi: 10.1126/sciadv.aba0398. Print 2020 Sep.

9. Reid Dylan A, Reed Patrick J, Schlachetzki Johannes CM, et al. Incorporation of a nucleoside analog maps genome repair sites in postmitotic human neurons. Science 2021 Apr 2;372(6537):91-94. https://doi: 10.1126/science.abb9032.

10. Berger Ralph J. Slow wave sleep, shallow torpor and hibernation: homologous states of diminished metabolism and body temperature. Biological Psychology 1984 Dec;19(3-4):305-26. https://doi: 10.1016/0301-0511(84)90045-0.

11. Silvani Alessandro, Cerri Matteo, Zoccoli Giovanna, Swoap Steven J. Is adenosine action common ground for NREM sleep, torpor, and other hypometabolic states? Physiology (Bethesda) 2018 May 1;33(3):182-196. doi: 10.1152/physiol.00007.2018.

12. Borbely Alexander A, Daan Serge, Wirz-Justice Anna, Deboer Tom. The two-process model of sleep regulation: a

reappraisal. Journal of Sleep Research 2016 Apr;25(2):131-43. https://doi: 10.1111/jsr.12371. Epub 2016 Jan 14.

13. Gagglioni Giulia, Maquet Pierre, Schmidt Christina, Dijk Derk-Jan, Vandewalle Giles. Neuroimaging, cognition, light and circadian rhythms. Frontiers in Systems Neuroscience 2014 Jul 8;8:126. https://doi: 10.3389/fnsys.2014.00126. eCollection 2014.

14. Garbazza Corrado, Benedetti Francesco. Genetic factors affecting seasonality, mood, and the circadian clock. Frontiers in Endocrinology 2018 Aug 23;9:481. https://doi: 10.3389/fendo.2018.00481. eCollection 2018.

15. Borbély, Alexander A. A two process model of sleep regulation. Human Neurobiology 1982;1(3):195-204.204.

16. Vanderwalle Giles, Archer Simon N, Wuillaume Catherine, et al. Functional magnetic resonance imaging-assessed brain responses during an executive task depend on interaction of sleep homeostasis, circadian phase, and PER3 genotype. The Journal of Neuroscience 2009 Jun 24;29(25):7948-56. https://doi: 10.1523/JNEUROSCI.0229-09.2009.

17. Spiegel Karine, Leproult Rachel, Van Cauter Eve. Impact of sleep debt on metabolic and endocrine function. Lancet 1999 Oct 23;354(9188):1435-9. https://doi: 10.1016/S0140-6736(99)01376-8.

18. Hudson Amanda N, Van Dongen Hans PA, Honn Kimberly A. Sleep deprivation, vigilant attention, and brain function: a review. Neuropsychopharmacology 2020 Jan;45(1):21-30. https://doi: 10.1038/s41386-019-0432-6. Epub 2019 Jun 8.

19. Gonzalez-Bernado Enrique, Russo Luca F, Valderrabano Esther, Fernandez Angel, Penteriani Vincenzo. Denning in brown bears. Ecology and Evolution 2020 May

25;10(13):6844-6862. https://doi: 10.1002/ece3.6372. eCollection 2020 Jul.

20. Archer Simon N, Schmidt Christina, Vandewalle Giles, Dijk Derk-Jan. Phenotyping of PER3 variants reveals widespread effects on circadian preference, sleep regulation, and health. Sleep Medicine Reviews 2018 Aug;40:109-126. https://doi: 10.1016/j.smrv.2017.10.008. Epub 2017 Nov 6.

21. Harding Edward C, Franks Nicholas P, Wisden William. The temperature dependence of sleep. Frontiers in Neuroscience 2019 Apr 24;13:336. doi: 10.3389/fnins.2019.00336. eCollection 2019.

22. Koroboki Eleni, Manios Efstathios, Psaltopoulou Theodora, et al. Circadian variation of blood pressure and heart rate in normotensives, white-coat, masked, treated and untreated hypertensives. Hellenic Journal of Cardiology 2012 Nov-Dec;53(6):432-8.

23. Kilduff Thomas S, Krilowicz Beverly, Milsom William K, Trachsel Lorenz, Wang Lawrence C. Sleep and mammalian hibernation: Homologous adaptations and homologous processes? Sleep 1993 Jun;16(4):372-86. https://doi: 10.1093/sleep/16.4.372.

24. Luppi Pierre-Herve, Fort Patrice. Neuroanatomical and neurochemical bases of vigilance states. Handbook of Experimental Pharmacology 2019;253:35-58. https://doi: 10.1007/164_2017_84.

25. Blanco Marina B, Dausmann Kathrin H, Faherty Sheena L, et al. Hibernation in a primate: does sleep occur? Royal Society Open Science 2016 Aug 10;3(8):160282. https://doi: 10.1098/rsos.160282. eCollection 2016 Aug.

26. Kayaba Momoko, Park Insung, Iwayama Kaito, et al. Energy metabolism differs between sleep stages and begins to increase prior to awakening. Metabolism. 2017 Apr;69:14-23. https://doi: 10.1016/j.metabol.2016.12.016. Epub 2017 Jan 4.

27. Girardeau Gabrielle, Lopes-do-Santos Vitor. Brain neural patterns and the memory function of sleep. Science 2021 Oct 28. https://doi: 10.1126/science.abi8370.

28. Achermann Peter, Dijk Derk-Jan, Brunner Daniel P, Borberly Alexander A. A model of human sleep homeostasis based on EEG slow-wave activity: quantitative comparison of data and simulations. Brain Research Bulletin 1993;31(1-2):97-113. https://doi: 10.1016/0361-9230(93)90016-5.

29. Heller Craig H, Ruby Norman F. Sleep and circadian rhythms in mammalian torpor. Annual Review of Physiology 2004;66:275-89. https://doi: 10.1146/annurev.physiol.66.032102.115313.

30. Ferrara Michele, De Gennaro Luigi. Going local: Insights from EEG and stereo-EEG studies of the human sleep-wake cycle. Current Topics in Medicinal Chemistry 2011;11(19):2423-37. https://doi: 10.2174/156802611797470268.

31. Sonntag Mandy, Arendt Thomas. Neuronal activity in the hibernating brain. Frontiers in Neuroanatomy 2019 Jul 9;13:71. https://doi: 10.3389/fnana.2019.00071. eCollection 2019.

32. Fernandez Guerro Antonio, Achermann Peter. Brain dynamics during sleep onset transition: An EEG source localization study. Neurobiology of Sleep and Circadian Rhythms 2018 Nov 28;6:24-34. https://doi: 10.1016/j.nbscr.2018.11.001. eCollection 2019 Jan.

33. Huang Zhi-Li, Urade Yoshihiro, Hayaishi Osamu. The role of adenosine in the regulation of sleep. Current Topics in Medicinal Chemistry 2011;11(8):1047-57. https://doi: 10.2174/156802611795347654.

34. Green Robert, Bjorness Theresa, Suzuki Ayako. The adenosine-mediated, neuronal-glial, homeostatic sleep response. Current Opinion in Neurobiology 2017

Jun;44:236-242. https://doi: 10.1016/j.conb.2017.05.015. Epub 2017 Jun 19.

35. Tupone Domenico, Madden Christopher J, Morrison Shaun F. Central activation of the A1 adenosine receptor (A1AR) induces a hypothermic, torpor-like state in the rat. Journal of Neuroscience 2013 Sep 4;33(36):14512-25. doi: 10.1523/JNEUROSCI.1980-13.2013.

36. Basheer Radhika, Strecker Robert E, Thakkar Mahesh M, McCarley Robert W. Adenosine and sleep-wake regulation. Progress in Neurobiology 2004 Aug;73(6):379-96. https://doi: 10.1016/j.pneurobio.2004.06.004.

37. Bjorness Theresa E, Kelly Christine L, Gao Tianshu, Poffenberger Virginia, Greene Robert W. Control and function of the homeostatic sleep response by adenosine A1 receptors. The Journal of Neuroscience 2009 Feb 4;29(5):1267-76. doi: 10.1523/JNEUROSCI.2942-08.2009.

38. Bjorness Theresa E, Greene Robert W. Adenosine and sleep. Adenosine and sleep. Current neuropharmacology 2009 Sep;7(3):238-45. https://doi: 10.2174/157015909789152182.

39. Jagannath Aart, Varga Norbert, Dallmann Robert, et al. Adenosine integrates light and sleep signalling for the regulation of circadian timing in mice. Nature Communications 2021 Apr 9;12(1):2113. https://doi: 10.1038/s41467-021-22179-z.

40. Purnell Benton, Murugan Madhuvika, Jani Raja, Boison Detlev. The good, the bad, and the deadly: Adenosinergic mechanisms underlying sudden unexpected death in epilepsy. Frontiers in Neuroscience 2021 Jul 12;15:708304. https://doi: 10.3389/fnins.2021.708304. eCollection 2021.

41. Boison Detlev. Adenosine as a neuromodulator in neurological diseases. Current Opinion in Pharmacology 2008 Feb;8(1):2-7. https://doi: 10.1016/j.coph.2007.09.002. Epub 2007 Oct 17.

42. Ely Stephen W, Berne Robert M. Protective effects of adenosine in myocardial ischemia. Circulation 1992 Mar;85(3):893-904. https://doi: 10.1161/01.cir.85.3.893.

43. Bouma Marjan G, van den Wilenberg Frans A, Buurman Wim A. The anti-inflammatory potential of adenosine in ischemia-reperfusion injury: established and putative beneficial actions of a retaliatory metabolite. Shock 1997 Nov;8(5):313-20. https://doi: 10.1097/00024382-199711000-00001.

44. Swoap Steven J. The pharmacology and molecular mechanisms underlying temperature regulation and torpor. Biochemical Pharmacology 2008 Oct 1;76(7):817-24. https://doi: 10.1016/j.bcp.2008.06.017. Epub 2008 Jul 3.

45. Borea Pier A, Gessi Stefania, Merighi Stefania, Vincenzi Fabrizio, Varani Katia. Pharmacology of adenosine receptors: The state of the art. Physiological Reviews 2018 Jul 1;98(3):1591-1625. https://doi: 10.1152/physrev.00049.2017.

46. Carta Sonia, Penco Federica, Lavieri Rosa, et al. Cell stress increases ATP release in NLRP3 inflammasome-mediated autoinflammatory diseases. Proceedings of the National Academy of Sciences of the USA 2015 Mar 3;112(9):2835-40. https://doi: 10.1073/pnas.1424741112. Epub 2015 Feb 17.

47. Magni Giulia, Ceruti Stefania. Adenosine signalling in autoimmune disorders. Pharmaceuticals (Basel) 2020 Sep 22;13(9):260. https://doi: 10.3390/ph13090260.

48. Soo Elizabeth, Welch Anthony, Marsh Christopher, McKay Dianne B. Molecular strategies used by hibernators: Potential therapeutic directions for ischemia reperfusion injury and preservation of human donor organs. Transplantation Reviews (Orlando) 2020 Jan;34(1):100514. https://doi: 10.1016/j.trre.2019.100514. Epub 2019 Oct 17.

49. Province Haley S, Xiao Cuiying, Mogul Allison S, et al. Activation of neuronal adenosine A1 receptors causes hypothermia through central and peripheral mechanisms. PLoS One 2020 Dec 16;15(12):e0243986. https://doi: 10.1371/journal.pone.0243986. eCollection 2020.

50. Soto Marion, Orliaguet Lucie, Reyzer Michelle L, Manier M Lisa, Caprioli Richard M, Kahn C Ronald. Pyruvate induces torpor in obese mice. Proceedings of the National Academy of the Sciences of the USA 2018 Jan 23;115(4):810-815. https://doi: 10.1073/pnas.1717507115. Epub 2018 Jan 8.

51. Yudkoff Marc, Daikhin Yevgeny, Horyn Oksana, Nissim Ilana, Itzhak Nissim. Ketosis and brain handling of glutamate, glutamine and GABA. Epilepsia 2008 Nov;49 Suppl 8(Suppl 8):73-5. https://doi: 10.1111/j.1528-1167.2008.01841.x.

52. Schwartz Michael D, Kilduff Thomas S. The neurobiology of sleep and wakefulness. The Psychiatric Clinics of North America 2015 Dec;38(4):615-44. https://doi: 10.1016/j.psc.2015.07.002. Epub 2015 Aug 28.

53. Rohr Kayla, Pancholi Harshida, Haider Shabi, et al. Seasonal plasticity in GABA A signaling is necessary for restoring phase synchrony in the master circadian clock network. Elife 2019 Nov 20;8:e49578. https://doi: 10.7554/eLife.49578.

54. Ono Daisuke, Honma Ken-Ichi, Yanagawa Yuchio, Yamanaka Akihiro, Honma Sato. Role of GABA in the regulation of the central circadian clock of the suprachiasmatic nucleus. The Journal of Physiological Sciences. 2018 Jul;68(4):333-343. https://doi: 10.1007/s12576-018-0604-x. Epub 2018 Mar 20.

55. McGrath Thomas, Baskerville Richard, Rogero Marcelo, Castell Linda. Emerging evidence for the widespread role of glutamatergic dysfunction in neuropsychiatric diseases. Nutrients 2022 Feb 22;14(5):917. https://doi: 10.3390/nu14050917.

56. Wehr Thomas A, Duncan Wallace C, Sher Leo, et al. A circadian signal of change of season in patients with seasonal affective disorder. Archives of General Psychiatry. 2001;58:1108–1114. https://doi: 10.1001/archpsyc.58.12.1108.

57. Czapski Grzegorz A, Stosznajder Joanna B. Glutamate and GABA in microglia-neuron cross-talk in Alzheimer's disease. International Journal of Molecular Sciences 2021 Oct 28;22(21):11677. https://doi: 10.3390/ijms222111677.

58. Morrison Shaun F, Kazuhiro Nakamura C. Central neural pathways for thermoregulation. Annual Review of Physiology 2019 Feb 10;81:285-308. https://doi: 10.1146/annurev-physiol-020518-114546. Epub 2018 Sep 26.

59. Tan Chan L, Cooke Elizabeth K, Leib David E, et al. Warm-sensitive neurons that control body temperature. Cell 2016 Sep 22;167(1):47-59.e15. doi: 10.1016/j.cell.2016.08.028. Epub 2016 Sep 8.

60. Esquifino, Ana I, Pandi-Perumal Seithikurippu R, Cardinaldi Daniel P. Circadian organization of the immune response: A role for melatonin. Clinical and Applied Immunology Reviews 2004 4:6:423-433. https://doi: 10.1016/j.cair.2004.08.002.

61. Srinivasan Venkataramanujan, Maestroni Georges JM, Cardinali Daniel, Esquifino Ana., Pandi-Perumal Seithikurippu R, Miller Steve. Melatonin, immune function and aging. Immunity and Ageing 2005 Nov 29;2:17. https://doi: 10.1186/1742-4933-2-17.

62. Tan Dun-Xian, Manchester Lucien C, Esteban-Zubero Eduardo, Zhou Zhou, Reiter Russel J. Melatonin as a potent and inducible endogenous antioxidant: synthesis and metabolism. Molecules 2015 Oct 16;20(10):18886-906. https://doi: 10.3390/molecules201018886.

63. Jung Christopher M, Melanson Edward L, Frydendall Emily J, Perreault Leigh, Eckel Robert H, Wright Kenneth P. Energy expenditure during sleep, sleep deprivation and sleep following sleep deprivation in adult humans. Journal of Physiology 2011 Jan 1;589(Pt 1):235-44. https://doi: 10.1113/jphysiol.2010.197517. Epub 2010 Nov 8.

64. Irwin Michael R, Vitiello Michael V. Implications of sleep disturbance and inflammation for Alzheimer's disease dementia. The Lancet. Neurology 2019 Mar;18(3):296-306. https://doi: 10.1016/S1474-4422(18)30450-2. Epub 2019 Jan 17.

65. Odintsova Tetiana A, Kopshak Oksana O. Sleep disorders in relapsing-remitting multiple sclerosis patients. Wiadomosci Lekarskie 2021;74(2):257-262.

66. Bertisch Suzanne M, Pollock Benjamin D, Mittleman Murray A, et al. Insomnia with objective short sleep duration and risk of incident cardiovascular disease and all-cause mortality: Sleep Heart Health Study. Sleep 2018 Jun 1;41(6):zsy047. https://doi: 10.1093/sleep/zsy047.

67. Buttner-Teleaga Antje, Kim Youn-Tae, Osel Tiziana, Richter Kneginja S. Sleep disorders in cancer-a systematic review. International Journal of Environmental Research and Public Health 2021 Nov 7;18(21):11696. https://doi: 10.3390/ijerph182111696.

68. Marjot Thomas, Ray David W, Williams Felicity R, Tomlinson Jeremy W, Armstrong Matthew J. Sleep and liver disease: a bidirectional relationship. The Lancet. Gastroenterology and Hepatology 2021 Oct;6(10):850-863. https://doi: 10.1016/S2468-1253(21)00169-2. Epub 2021 Jul 15.

69. Natale Patrizia, Ruospo Marinella, Saglimbene Valeria M, Palmer Suetonia C, Strippoli Giovanni FM. Interventions for improving sleep quality in people with chronic kidney disease. The Cochrane Database of Systematic Reviews 2019 May 26;5(5):CD012625. https://doi: 10.1002/14651858.CD012625.pub2.

70. North Brian J, Sinclair David A. The intersection between aging and cardiovascular disease. Circulation Research 2012 Apr 13;110(8):1097-108. https://doi: 10.1161/CIRCRESAHA.111.246876.

6. Internal Distress

1. Mangold Colleen A, Ishler Melissa J, Loreto Raquel G, Hazen Missy L, Hughes David P. Zombie ant death grip due to hypercontracted mandibular muscles. Journal of Experimental Biology 2019;222(Pt 14). https://doi:10.1242/jeb.200683.

2. Jarchum Irene, Pamer Eric G. Regulation of innate and adaptive immunity by the commensal microbiota. Current Opinion in Immunology 2011;23(3). https://doi:10.1016/j.coi.2011.03.001.

3. van de Guchte Maarten, Blottière Herve M, Doré Joel. Humans as holobionts: implications for prevention and therapy. Microbiome. 2018;6(1). https://doi:10.1186/s40168-018-0466-8.

4. Proal Amy D, Marshall Trevor G. Re-framing the theory of autoimmunity in the era of the microbiome: persistent pathogens, autoantibodies, and molecular mimicry. Discovery Medicine 2018;25(140). https://pubmed.ncbi.nlm.nih.gov/30021103/.

5. König Rahel S, Albrich Werner C, Kahlert Christian R, et al. The gut microbiome in myalgic encephalomyelitis (ME)/chronic fatigue syndrome (CFS). Frontiers in Immunology 2022;12. https://doi:10.3389/fimmu.2021.628741.

6. Salami Mahmoud. Interplay of good bacteria and central nervous system: Cognitive aspects and mechanistic considerations. Frontiers in Neuroscience 2021;15. https://doi:10.3389/fnins.2021.613120.

7. Smits Samuel A, Leach Jeff, Sonnenburg Erica D, et al. Seasonal cycling in the gut microbiome of the Hadza hunter-gatherers of Tanzania. Science 2017;357(6353). https://doi:10.1126/science.aan4834.

8. Sailani M Reza, Metwally Ahmed A, Zhou Wenyu, et al. Deep longitudinal multiomics profiling reveals two biological seasonal patterns in California. Nature Communications 2020;11(1). https://doi:10.1038/s41467-020-18758-1.

9. Medzhitov Ruslan, Schneider David S, Soares Miguel P. Disease tolerance as a defense strategy. Science 2012;335(6071). https://doi:10.1126/science.1214935.

10. Riera Romo Mario, Pérez-Martínez Dayana, Castillo Ferrer Camila. Innate immunity in vertebrates: an overview. Immunology 2016;148(2). https://doi:10.1111/imm.12597.

11. Connolly Emma, Hussell Tracy. The impact of type 1 interferons on alveolar macrophage tolerance and implications for host susceptibility to secondary bacterial pneumonia. Frontiers in Immunology 2020;11. https://doi:10.3389/fimmu.2020.00495.

12. Roquilly Antoine, McWilliam Hammish EG, Jacqueline Cedric, et al. Local modulation of antigen-presenting cell development after resolution of pneumonia induces long-term susceptibility to secondary infections. Immunity 2017;47(1). https://doi:10.1016/j.immuni.2017.06.021.

13. Basil Maria C, Levy Bruce D. Specialized pro-resolving mediators: endogenous regulators of infection and inflammation. Nature Reviews Immunology 2016;16(1). https://doi:10.1038/nri.2015.4.

14. Serhan Charles N, Chiang Nan, Van Dyke Thomas E. Resolving inflammation: dual anti-inflammatory and pro-resolution lipid mediators. Nature Reviews. Immunology 2008;8(5). https://doi:10.1038/nri2294.

15. Panigrahy Dipak, Gilligan Molly M, Huang Sui, et al. Inflammation resolution: a dual-pronged approach to averting cytokine storms in COVID-19? Cancer Metastasis Reviews 2020;39(2). https://doi:10.1007/s10555-020-09889-4.

16. McCarville Justin L, Ayres Janelle S. Disease tolerance: concept and mechanisms. Current Opinion in Immunology 2018;50. https://doi:10.1016/j.coi.2017.12.003.

17. López-Collazo Eduardo, del Fresno Carlos. Pathophysiology of endotoxin tolerance: mechanisms and clinical consequences. Critical Care 2013;17(6). https://doi:10.1186/cc13110.

18. Swedo Susan, Leckman James, Rose Noel R. From research subgroup to clinical syndrome: Modifying the PANDAS criteria to describe PANS (Pediatric Acute-onset Neuropsychiatric Syndrome). Pediatrics & Therapeutics 2012;2. https://doi:10.4172/2161-0665.1000113.

19. Underhill Rosemary A. Myalgic encephalomyelitis, chronic fatigue syndrome: An infectious disease. Medical Hypotheses 2015;85(6). https://doi:10.1016/j.mehy.2015.10.011.

20. Orlovska Sonja, Vestergaard Claus H, Bech Bodil H, Nordentoft Merete, Vestergaard Mogens, Benros Michael E. Association of streptococcal throat infection with mental disorders: Testing key aspects of the PANDAS hypothesis in a nationwide study. Journal of the American Medical Association Psychiatry 2017;74(7). https://doi:10.1001/jamapsychiatry.2017.0995.

21. Bessen Debra E. Population biology of the human restricted pathogen, Streptococcus Pyogenes. Infection Genetics and Evolution 2009;9(4). https://doi.10.1016/j.meegid.2009.03.002.

22. Walker Mark J, Barnett Timothy C, McArthur Jason D, et al. Disease manifestations and pathogenic mechanisms of

Group A Streptococcus. Clinical Microbiology Reviews 2014;27(2). https://doi:10.1128/CMR.00101-13.

23. Baruch Moshe, Hertzog Baruch B, Ravins Miriam, et al. Induction of endoplasmic reticulum stress and unfolded protein response constitutes a pathogenic strategy of group A streptococcus. Frontiers in Cellular Infection and Microbiology 2014;4. https://doi:10.3389/fcimb.2014.00105.

24. Soderholm Amelia T, Barnett Timothy C, Sweet Matthew J, Walker Mark J. Group A streptococcal pharyngitis: Immune responses involved in bacterial clearance and GAS-associated immunopathologies. Journal of Leukocyte Biology 2018;103(2). https://doi:10.1189/jlb.4MR0617-227RR.

25. Valderrama J Andre, Nizet Victor. Group A streptococcus encounters with host macrophages. Future Microbiology 2018;13(1). https://doi.10.2217/fmb-2107-0142.

26. Sika-Paotonu Dianne, Beaton Andrea, Raghu Aparna, Steer Andrew, Carapetis Jonathan. Acute rheumatic fever and rheumatic disease. In, Streptococcus Pyogenes: Basic Biology to Clinical Manifestations, Ferretti Joseph J, Stevens Dennis L, Fischetti Vincent A, eds. Oklahoma City (OK): University of Oklahoma Health Sciences Center; 2016. https://www.ncbi.nlm.nih.gov/books/NBK333424/.

27. Dop Dalia, Marcu Iulia R, Padureanu Rodica, Niculescu Carmen E, Padureanu Vlad. Pediatric autoimmune neuropsychiatric disorders associated with streptococcal infections. Experimental and Therapeutic Medicine 2021;21(1):94. https://doi:10.3892/etm.2020.9526.

28. Schloder Janine, Shahneh Fatemeh, Schneider Franz-Joseph, Wieschendorf Bjorn. Boosting regulatory T cell function for the treatment of autoimmune diseases - That's only half the battle! Frontiers in Immunology 2022 Aug 10;13:973813. https://doi: 10.3389/fimmu.2022.973813. eCollection 2022.

29. Houen Gunnar, Trier Nicole H, Frederiksen Jette L. Epstein-Barr virus and multiple sclerosis. Frontiers in Immunology 2020;11:587078. https://doi:10.3389/fimmu.2020.587078.

30. Bjornevik Kjetil, Cortese Marianna Healy Brian C, et al. Longitudinal analysis reveals high prevalence of Epstein-Barr virus associated with multiple sclerosis Science 2022 Jan 21;375(6578):296-301. https://doi: 10.1126/science.abj8222.

31. Poulain Daniel. Candida albicans, plasticity and pathogenesis. Critical Reviews in Microbiology 2015;41(2). https://doi:10.3109/1040841X.2013.813904.

32. Wang Yan. Looking into Candida albicans infection, host response, and antifungal strategies. Virulence 2015;6(4). https://doi:10.1080/21505594.2014.1000752.

33. Wallis Amy, Ball Michelle, Butt Henry, et al. Open-label pilot for treatment targeting gut dysbiosis in myalgic encephalomyelitis/chronic fatigue syndrome: neuropsychological symptoms and sex comparisons. Journal of Translational Medicine 2018;16(1). https://doi:10.1186/s12967-018-1392-z.

34. Donnachie Ewan Schneider Antonius, Enck Paul. Comorbidities of patients with functional somatic syndromes before, during and after first diagnosis: A population-based study using Bavarian Routine Data. Scientific Reports 2020;10(1):9810. https://doi:10.1038/s41598-020-66685-4.

35. Buonsenso Danilo, Di Gennaro Leonardo, De Rose Cristina, et al. Long-term outcomes of pediatric infections: from traditional infectious diseases to long Covid. Future Microbiology 2022;17. https://doi:10.2217/fmb-2022-0031.

36. Brown Guy C. The endotoxin hypothesis of neurodegeneration. Journal of Neuroinflammation 2019;16(1). https://doi:10.1186/s12974-019-1564-7.

37. Beurel Eleonore. HDAC6 regulates LPS-tolerance in astrocytes. PLoS One. 2011;6(10):e25804. https://doi:10.1371/journal.pone.0025804.

38. Rogovskii Vladimir. Immune tolerance as the physiologic counterpart of chronic inflammation. Frontiers in Immunology 2020 Sep 30;11:2061. https://doi: 10.3389/fimmu.2020.02061. eCollection 2020.

7. Chronic Distress

1. Cannon Walter B. Bodily Changes in Pain, Hunger, Fear and Rage. New York, NY:D. Appleton and Company; 1925.

2. Selye, Hans. Stress and the general adaptation syndrome. British Medical Journal 1950 Jun 17; 1(4667): 1383–1392. https://doi:10.1136/bmj.1.4667.1383.

3. Dhabhar Firdaus S, McEwen Bruce S. Acute stress enhances while chronic stress suppresses cell-mediated immunity in vivo: a potential role for leukocyte trafficking. Brain Behavior and Immunity 1997 Dec;11(4):286-306. https://doi: 10.1006/brbi.1997.0508.

4. McEwen Bruce S. Neurobiological and systemic effects of chronic stress. Chronic Stress 2017 Jan-Dec;1:2470547017692328. https://doi: 10.1177/2470547017692328. Epub 2017 Apr 10.

5. Armour J. Andrew, Ardell Jeffrey L. Basic and Clinical Neurocardiology. New York, NY: Oxford University Press; 2004.

6. Reardon Colin, Murray Kaitlin, Lomax Alan E. Neuroimmune communication in health and disease. Physiological Reviews 2018 Oct 1;98(4):2287-2316. https://doi: 10.1152/physrev.00035.2017.

7. Pavlov Valentin A, Tracey Kevin J. The vagus nerve and the inflammatory reflex–linking immunity and metabolism. Nature Reviews Endocrinology 2012 Dec;8(12):743-54. https://doi: 10.1038/nrendo.2012.189.

8. Thayer Julian F, Lane Richard D. Claude Bernard and the heart-brain connection: Further elaboration of a model of neurovisceral integration. Neuroscience and Biobehavioral Reviews 2009 Feb;33(2):81-8. https://doi: 10.1016/j.neubiorev.2008.08.004. Epub 2008 Aug 13.

9. Godoy Livea D, Rossignoli Mattheus T, Delfino-Pereira Polianna, Garcia-Cairasco Norberto, de Lima Umeoka Eduardo H. A comprehensive overview on stress neurobiology: Basic concepts and clinical implications Frontiers in Behavioral Neuroscience 2018 Jul 3;12:127. https://doi: 10.3389/fnbeh.2018.00127. eCollection 2018.

10. Benarroch Eduardo E. Physiology and pathophysiology of the autonomic nervous system. Continuum 2020 Feb;26(1):12-24. https://doi: 10.1212/CON.0000000000000817.

11. Karemaker John M. An introduction into autonomic nervous function. Physiological measurement 2017 May;38(5):R89-R118. https://doi: 10.1088/1361-6579/aa6782. Epub 2017 Mar 17.

12. Arrais Rocha Eduardo, Mehta Niraj, Tavora-Mehta MZP et al. Dysautonomia: A forgotten condition - Part 1. Arquivos Brasileiros de Cardiologia 2021 Apr;116(4):814-835. https://doi: 10.36660/abc.20200420.

13. Agorastos Agorastos, Olff Miranda. Sleep, circadian system and traumatic stress. European Journal of Psychotraumatology 2021 Sep 28;12(1):1956746. https://doi: 10.1080/20008198.2021.1956746. eCollection 2021.

14. Thayer Julian F, Yamamoto Shelby S, Brosschot Jos F. The relationship of autonomic imbalance, heart rate variability and cardiovascular disease risk factors. International Journal of

Cardiology 2010 May 28;141(2):122-31. doi: 10.1016/j.ijcard.2009.09.543. Epub 2009 Nov 11.

15. Nakano Tomoya, Onoue Kenji, Nakada Yasuki, et al. Alteration of β-adrenoceptor signaling in left ventricle of acute phase takotsubo syndrome: a human study. Scientific Reports 2018 Aug 24;8(1):12731. https://doi: 10.1038/s41598-018-31034-z.

16. Sanchez John MS, McNally J Scott, Cortez Melissa M, Hemp James, Pace Laura A, Clardy Stacey L. Neuroimmunogastroenterology: At the interface of neuroimmunology and gastroenterology. Frontiers in Neurology 2020 Jul 31;11:787. https://doi: 10.3389/fneur.2020.00787. eCollection 2020.

17. Carrara Marta, Ferrario Manuela, Bollen Pinto Bernardo, Herpain Antoine. The autonomic nervous system in septic shock and its role as a future therapeutic target: a narrative review. Annals of Intensive Care 2021 May 17;11(1):80. https://doi: 10.1186/s13613-021-00869-7.

18. Chaves Tiago, Fazekas Csilla L, Horvath Krisztina, et al. Stress adaptation and the brainstem with focus on corticotropin-releasing hormone. International Journal of Molecular Sciences 2021 Aug 23;22(16):9090. https://doi: 10.3390/ijms22169090.

19. Sato Kohji. Why is prepulse inhibition disrupted in schizophrenia? Medical Hypotheses 2020 Oct;143:109901. https://doi: 10.1016/j.mehy.2020.109901. Epub 2020 May 30.

20. Ulrich-Lai Yvonne, Herman James P. Neural regulation of endocrine and autonomic stress responses. Nature Reviews. Neuroscience 2009 Jun;10(6):397-409. https://doi: 10.1038/nrn2647.

21. Kim Hei S, Yosipovitch Gil. An aberrant parasympathetic response: a new perspective linking chronic stress and itch. Experimental Dermatology 2013 Apr;22(4):239-44. https://doi: 10.1111/exd.12070.

22. Porges Stephen W. The Polyvagal Theory: Neurophysiological Foundations of Emotions, Attachment, Communication, and Self-regulation. New York, NY: W.W. Norton and Company; 2011.

23. Kleiger Robert E, Stein Phyllis K, Bigger Jr. J Thomas. Heart rate variability: measurement and clinical utility. Annals of Noninvasive Electrocardiology 2005 Jan;10(1):88-101. https://doi: 10.1111/j.1542-474X.2005.10101.x.

24. Benjamin Beatrice R. Valstad, Mathias Elvsåshagen Torbjørn, et al. Heart rate variability is associated with disease severity in psychosis spectrum disorders. Progress in Neuro-Psychopharmacology and Biological Psychiatry 2021 Dec 20;111:110108. https://doi: 10.1016/j.pnpbp.2020.110108. Epub 2020 Sep 15.

25. Huikuri Heikki V, Makikallio Timo H. Heart rate variability in ischemic heart disease. Autonomic Neuroscience 2001 Jul 20;90(1-2):95-101. https://doi: 10.1016/S1566-0702(01)00273-9.

26. Orjatsalo Maija, Alakuijala Anniina, Partinen Markku. Heart rate variability in head-up tilt tests in adolescent postural tachycardia syndrome patients. Frontiers in Neuroscience 2020 Aug 11;14:725. https://doi: 10.3389/fnins.2020.00725. eCollection 2020.

27. Picard Martin, McEwen Bruce S. Psychological stress and mitochondria: A conceptual framework. Psychosomatic Medicine 018 Feb/Mar;80(2):126-140. https://doi: 10.1097/PSY.0000000000000544.

28. Du Yuxin, Demillard Laurie J, Ren Jun. Catecholamine-induced cardiotoxicity: A critical element in the pathophysiology of stroke-induced heart injury. Life Sciences 2021 Dec 15;287:120106. https://doi: 10.1016/j.lfs.2021.120106. Epub 2021 Oct 28.

29. Kubzansky Laura D, Adler Gail K. Aldosterone: a forgotten mediator of the relationship between psychological stress and heart disease. Neuroscience and Biobehavioral Reviews 2010 Jan;34(1):80-6. https://doi: 10.1016/j.neubiorev.2009.07.005. Epub 2009 Jul 22.

30. Rajbhandari Abha K, Bakshi Vaishali P. Repeated norepinephrine receptor stimulation in the bed nucleus of the stria terminalis [BNST] induces sensorimotor gating deficits via corticotropin releasing factor. Neuropharmacology 2020 Aug 1;172:108090. https://doi: 10.1016/j.neuropharm.2020.108090. Epub 2020 Apr 29.

31. Lynch James H, Mulvaney Sean W, Kim Eugene H, de Leeuw Jason B, Schroeder Matthew J, Kane Shawn F. Effect of stellate ganglion block on specific symptom clusters for treatment of post-traumatic stress disorder. Military Medicine 2016 Sep;181(9):1135-41. https://doi: 10.7205/MILMED-D-15-00518.

32. Oster H. The interplay between stress, circadian clocks, and energy metabolism. The Journal of Endocrinology 2020 Oct;247(1):R13-R25. https://doi: 10.1530/JOE-20-0124.

33. Carroll Douglas, Ginty Annie T, Whittaker Anna C, Lovallo William R, de Rooij Susanne R. The behavioural, cognitive, and neural corollaries of blunted cardiovascular and cortisol reactions to acute psychological stress. Neuroscience and Biobehavioral Reviews 2017 Jun;77:74-86. https://doi: 10.1016/j.neubiorev.2017.02.025. Epub 2017 Feb 27.

34. Basil Maria, Levy Bruce. Specialized pro-resolving mediators: endogenous regulators of infection and inflammation. Nature Reviews. Immunology 2016 Jan;16(1):51-67. https://doi: 10.1038/nri.2015.4. Epub 2015 Dec 21.

35. Fredman Gabriella, Spite Matthew. Specialized pro-resolving mediators in cardiovascular diseases. Molecular

Aspects of Medicine 2017 Dec;58:65-71. https://doi: 10.1016/j.mam.2017.02.003. Epub 2017 Feb 28.

36. Dhabhar Firdaus. The Short-Term Stress Response – Mother Nature's Mechanism for Enhancing Protection and Performance Under Conditions of Threat, Challenge, and Opportunity. Frontiers in Neuroendocrinology 2018 Apr; 49: 175–192.

37. Rogovskii Vladimir. Immune tolerance as the physiologic counterpart of chronic inflammation. Frontiers in Immunology 2020 Sep 30;11:2061. https://doi: 10.3389/fimmu.2020.02061. eCollection 2020.

38. Gallo Jiri, Raska Milan, Kriegova Eva, Goodman Stuart B. Inflammation and its resolution and the musculoskeletal system. Journal of Orthopaedic Translation 2021 Apr 2;12:664457. https://doi: 10.3389/fimmu.2021.664457. eCollection 2021.

39. Bianchi Marco E. DAMPs, PAMPs and alarmins: all we need to know about danger. Journal of Leukocyte Biology 2007 Jan;81(1):1-5. https://doi: 10.1189/jlb.0306164. Epub 2006 Oct 10.

40. Matzinger Polly, Kamala Tirumalai. Tissue-based class control: the other side of tolerance. Nature Reviews. Immunology 2011 Mar;11(3):221-30. https://doi: 10.1038/nri2940.

41. Placek Katarzyna, Schultze Joachim L, Aschenbrenner Anna C. Epigenetic reprogramming of immune cells in injury, repair, and resolution. The Journal of Clinical Investigation 2019 Jul 22;129(8):2994-3005. https://doi: 10.1172/JCI124619.

42. Naviaux Robert K. Incomplete healing as a cause of aging: The role of mitochondria and the cell danger response. Biology (Basel) 2019 May 11;8(2):27. https://doi: 10.3390/biology8020027.

43. Osimo Emanuele F, Baxter Luke J, Lewis Glyn, Jones Peter B. Khandaker Golam M. Prevalence of low-grade inflammation in depression: a systematic review and meta-analysis of CRP levels. Psychological Medicine 2019 Sep;49(12):1958-1970. https://doi: 10.1017/S0033291719001454. Epub 2019 Jul 1.

44. Novakovic Boris, Habibi Ehsan, Wang Shuang-Yin, et al. B-glucan reverses the epigenetic state of LPS-induced immunological tolerance. Cell 2016 Nov 17;167(5):1354-1368.e14. https://doi: 10.1016/j.cell.2016.09.034.

45. Zhou Yue, Chi Jingwei, Lv Wensham, Wang Yangang. Obesity and diabetes as high-risk factors fro severe coronavirus disease 2019 (Covid-19). Diabetes Metabolism Research Reviews 2021 Feb;37(2):e3377. https://doi: 10.1002/dmrr.3377. Epub 2020 Jul 20.

8. Chronic Distress and the Heart

1. Sato Masahito, Fujita Satoru, Saito Atushi, et al. Increased incidence of transient left ventricular apical ballooning (so-called "Takotsubo" cardiomyopathy) after the mid-Niigata Prefecture earthquake. Circulation Journal 2006 Aug;70(8):947-53. https://doi: 10.1253/circj.70.947.

2. Kloner Robert A. Stunned and hibernating myocardium: Where are we nearly 4 decades later? Journal of the American Heart Association 2020 Feb 4;9(3):e015502. https://doi: 10.1161/JAHA.119.015502. Epub 2020 Feb 4.

3. Boyd Brenton, Solh Tia. Takotsubo: Review of broken heart syndrome. Journal of the American Academy of Physician Assistants 2020 Mar;33(3):24-29. https://doi: 10.1097/01.JAA.0000654368.35241.fc.

4. Paur Helen, Wright Peter T, Sikkei Markus B, et al. High levels of circulating epinephrine trigger apical cardiodepression in a β2-adrenergic receptor/Gi-dependent manner: a new model of Takotsubo cardiomyopathy

Circulation 2012 Aug 7;126(6):697-706. https://doi: 10.1161/CIRCULATIONAHA.112.111591. Epub 2012 Jun 25.

5. Norcliffe-Kaufmann Lucy, Kaufmann Horacio, Martinez Martinez, Katz Astuart D, Tully Lisa, Reynolds Harmony R. Autonomic findings in Takotsubo cardiomyopathy. The American Journal of Cardiology 2016 Jan 15;117(2):206-13. https://doi: 10.1016/j.amjcard.2015.10.028. Epub 2015 Nov 5.

6. Brazdil Vojtech, Kala Petr, Hudec Martin. The role of central autonomic nervous system dysfunction in Takotsubo syndrome: a systematic review. Clinical Autonomic Research 2022 Feb;32(1):9-17. https://doi: 10.1007/s10286-021-00844-z. Epub 2022 Jan 8.

7. Templin Christian, Ghadri Jelena R, Diekmann Johanna, et al. Clinical features and outcomes of Takotsubo (stress) cardiomyopathy. New England Journal of Medicine 2015 Sep 3;373(10):929-38. https://doi: 10.1056/NEJMoa1406761.

8. Rahimtoola Shahbudin H. The hibernating myocardium. American Heart Journal 1989 Jan;117(1):211-21. doi: 10.1016/0002-8703(89)90685-6.

9. Biso Sylvia, Wongrakpanich Supakanya, Agrawai Akanksha, Yadlapati, Kishlyansky Marina, Figueredo Vincent. A review of neurogenic stunned myocardium. Cardiovascular Psychiatry and Neurology 2017;2017:5842182. https://doi: 10.1155/2017/5842182. Epub 2017 Aug 10.

10. Schotola Hanna, Toischer Karl, Popov Aron F et al. Mild metabolic acidosis impairs the B-adrenergic response in isolated human failing myocardium. Critical Care 2012 Aug 13;16(4):R153. https://doi: 10.1186/cc11468.

11. Adam Clement, Paolini Lea, Gueguen Naig, et al. Acetoacetate protects macrophages from lactic acidosis-induced mitochondrial dysfunction by metabolic reprograming. Nature Communications 2021 Dec 8;12(1):7115. https://doi: 10.1038/s41467-021-27426-x.

12. Kaplan Joel A, Guffin Anita V, Yin Andrew. The effects of metabolic acidosis and alkalosis on the response to sympathomimetic drugs in dogs. Journal of Cardiothoracic Anesthesia 1988 Aug;2(4):481-7. https://doi: 10.1016/0888-6296(88)90229-3.

13. Fischesser Demetria M, Bo Bin, Benton Rachel P, Su Haili, Jahanpanah Newsha, Haworth Kevin J. Controlling reperfusion injury with controlled reperfusion: Historical perspectives and new paradigms. Journal of Cardiovascular Pharmacology and Therapeutics 2021 Nov;26(6):504-523. https://doi: 10.1177/10742484211046674. Epub 2021 Sep 17.

14. Hussain Afthab, Karjian Patricia, Maddock Helen. The role of nitric oxide in A3 adenosine receptor-mediated cardioprotection. Autonomic and Autacoid Pharmacology 2009 Jul;29(3):97-104. https://doi: 10.1111/j.1474-8673.2009.00438.x.

15. Ritterhoff Julia, Tian Rong. Metabolism in cardiomyopathy: Every substrate matters. Cardiovascular Research 2017 Mar 15;113(4):411-421. https://doi: 10.1093/cvr/cvx017.

16. Zhou Bo, Tian Rong. Mitochondrial dysfunction in pathophysiology of heart failure. The Journal of Clinical Investigation 2018 Aug 31;128(9):3716-3726. https://doi: 10.1172/JCI120849. Epub 2018 Aug 20.

17. Beuchel Carl, Dittrich Julia, Pott Janne, et al. Blood metabolite profiles reflect changes in energy metabolism in heart failure. Metabolites 2022 Feb 27;12(3):216. https://doi: 10.3390/metabo12030216.

18. Guvakov Dmitri, Bezinover Dmitri, Lomivorotov Vladimir V, et al. The "Ice Age" in cardiac surgery: Evolution of the "Siberian" method of brain protection during deep hypothermic perfusionless circulatory arrest. The Journal of Cardiothoracic and Vascular Anesthesia 2019

Dec;33(12):3366-3374. https://doi: 10.1053/j.jvca.2019.04.001. Epub 2019 Apr 18.

19. Arrich Jasmin, Holzer Michael, Havel Christof, Mullner Marcus, Herkner Harald. Hypothermia for neuroprotection in adults after cardiopulmonary resuscitation. The Cochrane Database of Systematic Reviews 2016 Feb 15;2(2):CD004128. https://doi: 10.1002/14651858.CD004128.pub4.

20. Morris Gerwyn, Berk Michael, Walder Ken, Maes Michael. Central pathways causing fatigue in neuroinflammatory and autoimmune illnesses. BMC Medicine 2015 Feb 6;13:28. https://doi: 10.1186/s12916-014-0259-2.

21. Maes Michael, Twisk Frank N. Why myalgic encephalomyelitis/chronic fatigue syndrome (ME/CFS) may kill you: disorders in the inflammatory and oxidative and nitrosative stress (IO&NS) pathways may explain cardiovascular disorders in ME/CFS. Neuroendocrinology Letters 2009;30(6):677-93.

22. Bested Alison C, Marshall Lynn M.. Review of myalgic encephalomyelitis/chronic fatigue syndrome: an evidence-based approach to diagnosis and management by clinicians. Reviews on Environmental Health 2015;30(4):223-49. doi: 10.1515/reveh-2015-0026.

23. Fukuda Keiji, Straus Stephen E, Hickie Ian, et al. The chronic fatigue syndrome: A comprehensive approach to its definition and study. Annals of Internal Medicine 1994 Dec 15;121(12):953-9. https://doi: 10.7326/0003-4819-121-12-199412150-00009.

24. Mole Chris. Chronic fatigue syndrome - a personal story. https://www.healthinformation.co.nz, accessed 06/14/2022.

25. Sarah. Lunchtime Live. https://www.fatiguetalk.com, accessed 06/04/2022.

26. Vastag Brian. I'm disabled. Can the NIH spare a few dimes? The Washington Post July 20, 2015, accessed 06/04/2022.

9. Chronic Fatigue Syndrome

1. Morris Gerwyn, Maes Michael, Berk Michael, Puri Basant K. Myalgic encephalomyelitis or chronic fatigue syndrome: how could the illness develop? Metabolic Brain Disease 2019 Apr;34(2):385-415. https://doi: 10.1007/s11011-019-0388-6. Epub 2019 Feb 13.

2. Jason Leonard A, Sunnquist Madison, Brown Abigail, Reed Jordan. Defining essential features of myalgic encephalomyelitis and chronic fatigue syndrome. Journal of Human Behavior in the Social Environment 2015;25(6):657-674. https://doi: 10.1080/10911359.2015.1011256. Epub 2015 May 6.

3. Bested Alison C, Marshall Lynn M.. Review of myalgic encephalomyelitis/chronic fatigue syndrome: an evidence-based approach to diagnosis and management by clinicians. Reviews on Environmental Health 2015;30(4):223-49. doi: 10.1515/reveh-2015-0026.

4. Wirth Klaus, Scheibenbogen Carmen. A Unifying Hypothesis of the pathophysiology of myalgic encephalomyelitis/chronic fatigue syndrome (ME/CFS): Recognitions from the finding of autoantibodies against ß2-adrenergic receptors. Autoimmunity Reviews 2020 Jun;19(6):102527. https://doi: 10.1016/j.autrev.2020.102527. Epub 2020 Apr 1.

5. Lemle Marian D. Hypothesis: Chronic fatigue syndrome is caused by dysregulation of hydrogen sulfide metabolism. Medical Hypotheses 2009 Jan;72(1):108-9. https://doi: 10.1016/j.mehy.2008.08.003. Epub 2008 Sep 16.

6. Johnson Cort. The core problem in chronic fatigue syndrome identified? Naviaux's metabolomics study breaks

fresh ground. In, HealthRising:Finding Answers for ME/CFS and FM 2016 Sept 1. https://www.healthrising.org, accessed January 31, 2020.

7. Soo Elizabeth, Welch Anthony, Marsh Christopher, McKay Dianne B. Molecular strategies used by hibernators: Potential therapeutic directions for ischemia reperfusion injury and preservation of human donor organs. Transplantation Reviews (Orlando) 2020 Jan;34(1):100514. https://doi: 10.1016/j.trre.2019.100514. Epub 2019 Oct 17.

8. Anderson George, Maes Michael. Mitochondria and immunity in chronic fatigue syndrome. Progress in Neuropsychopharmacology and Biological Psychiatry 2020 Dec 20;103:109976. htps://doi: 10.1016/j.pnpbp.2020.109976. Epub 2020 May 26.

9. Fernandez-Guerra Paula, Gonzalez-Ebsen Ana C, Boonen Susanne E, et al. Bioenergetic and proteomic profiling of immune cells in myalgic encephalomyelitis/chronic fatigue syndrome patients: An exploratory study. Biomolecules 2021 Jun 29;11(7):961. https://doi: 10.3390/biom11070961.

10. Naviaux Robert K, Naviaux Jane C, Li Kefeng, et al. Metabolic features of chronic fatigue syndrome. Proceedings of the National Academy of Sciences of the USA 2016 Sep 13;113(37):E5472-80. https://doi: 10.1073/pnas.1607571113. Epub 2016 Aug 29.

11. Myhill Sarah, Booth Norman E, McLaren-Howard John. Chronic fatigue syndrome and mitochondrial dysfunction. International Journal of Clinical and Experimental Medicine 2009;2(1):1-16. Epub 2009 Jan 15.

12. Brown Audrey E, Dibnah Beth, Fisher Emily, Newton Julia L, Walker Mark. Pharmacological activation of AMPK and glucose uptake in cultured human skeletal muscle cells from patients with ME/CFS. Bioscience Reports 2018 May 8;38(3):BSR20180242. https://doi: 10.1042/BSR20180242. Print 2018 Jun 29.

13. Germain Arnaud, Ruppert David, Levine Susan M, Hanson Maureen R. Metabolic profiling of a myalgic encephalomyelitis/chronic fatigue syndrome discovery cohort reveals disturbances in fatty acid and lipid metabolism. Molecular Biosystems 2017 Jan 31;13(2):371-379. https://doi: 10.1039/c6mb00600k.

14. Tomas Cara, Elson Joanna L, Newton Julia L, Walker Mark. Substrate utilisation of cultured skeletal muscle cells in patients with CFS. Scientific Reports 2020 Oct 26;10(1):18232. https://doi: 10.1038/s41598-020-75406-w.

15. Naviaux Robert K. Oxidative shielding or oxidative stress? The Journal of Pharmacology and Experimental Therapeutics 2012 Sep;342(3):608-18. doi: 10.1124/jpet.112.192120. Epub 2012 Jun 13.

16. Maes Michael, Twisk Frank N. Why myalgic encephalomyelitis/chronic fatigue syndrome (ME/CFS) may kill you: disorders in the inflammatory and oxidative and nitrosative stress (IO&NS) pathways may explain cardiovascular disorders in ME/CFS. Neuroendocrinology Letters 2009;30(6):677-93.

17. Dantzer Robert. Cytokine, sickness behavior, and depression. Immunology and Allergy Clinics of North America 2009 May;29(2):247-64. https://doi: 10.1016/j.iac.2009.02.002.

18. Miller Andrew H, Maletic Vladimir, Raison Charles L. Inflammation and its discontents: the role of cytokines in the pathophysiology of major depression. Biological Psychiatry 2009 May 1;65(9):732-41. https://doi: 10.1016/j.biopsych.2008.11.029. Epub 2009 Jan 15.

19. Jin Yang, Sun Li H, Yang Wei, Cui Ran J, Xu Song B. The role of BDNF in the neuroimmune axis regulation of mood disorders. Frontiers in Neurology 2019 Jun 4;10:515. doi: 10.3389/fneur.2019.00515. eCollection 2019.

20. Shanahan Catherine. Deep Nutrition: Why Your Genes Need Traditional Food. Lawai HI: Big Box Books; 2018.

21. Reiter Russel J, Ma Qiang, Sharma Ramaswamy. Melatonin in mitochondria: mitigating clear and present dangers. Physiology (Bethesda) 2020 Mar 1;35(2):86-95. https://doi: 10.1152/physiol.00034.2019.

22. Murphy Brennah, Bhattacharya Resham, Mukherjee Priyabrata. Hydrogen sulfide signaling in mitochondria and disease. The FASEB Journal 2019 Dec;33(12):13098-13125. doi: 10.1096/fj.201901304R. Epub 2019 Oct 24.

23. Nathan Neil. Toxic: Heal Your Body. Las Vegas, NV: Victory Belt Publishing, Inc.; 2018.

24. Husebye Eystein S, Pearce Simon H, Krone Nils P, Kampe Olle. Adrenal insufficiency. Lancet 2021 Feb 13;397(10274):613-629. https://doi: 10.1016/S0140-6736(21)00136-7. Epub 2021 Jan 20.

25. Morris Gerwyn, Maes Michael. A neuro-immune model of myalgic encephalomyelitis/chronic fatigue syndrome. Metabolic Brain Disease 2013 Dec;28(4):523-40. https://doi: 10.1007/s11011-012-9324-8. Epub 2012 Jun 21.

26. Sotzny Franziska, Blanco Julia, Capelli Enrica, et al. Myalgic encephalomyelitis/chronic fatigue syndrome - Evidence for an autoimmune disease. Autoimmunity Reviews 2018 Jun;17(6):601-609. https://doi: 10.1016/j.autrev.2018.01.009. Epub 2018 Apr 7.

27. Morris Gerwyn, Berk Michael, Galecki Piotr, Maes Michael. The emerging role of autoimmunity in myalgic encephalomyelitis/chronic fatigue syndrome (ME/cfs). Molecular Neurobiology 2014 Apr;49(2):741-56. https://doi: 10.1007/s12035-013-8553-0. Epub 2013 Sep 26.

28. Berg David, Berg Lois H., Couvaras John, Harrison Hailey. Chronic fatigue syndrome and/or fibromyalgia as a variation of antiphospholipid antibody syndrome: An explanatory model and approach to laboratory diagnosis. Blood Coagulation and Fibrinolysis 1999;10:435–438. https://doi: 10.1097/00001721-199910000-00006.

29. Hokama Yoshitsugi, Campora Cara E, Hara Cynthia, Kuribayashi Tina, Huynh Diana L, Yabusaki Kenichi. Anticardiolipin antibodies in the sera of patients with diagnosed chronic fatigue syndrome. Journal of Clinical Laboratory Analysis 2009;23:210–212. https://doi: 10.1002/jcla.20325.

30. Scherbakov Nadja, Szklarski Marvin, Hartwig Jelka, et al. Peripheral endothelial dysfunction in myalgic encephalomyelitis/chronic fatigue syndrome. ESC Heart Failure 2020 Jun;7(3):1064-1071. https://doi: 10.1002/ehf2.12633. Epub 2020 Mar 10.

31. Yoshiuchi Kazuhiro, Farkas Jeffrey, Natelson Benjamin H. Patients with chronic fatigue syndrome have reduced absolute cortical blood flow. Clinical Physiology and Functional Imaging 2006 Mar;26(2):83-6. doi: 10.1111/j.1475-097X.2006.00649.x.

32. Conti Pio, Gallenga Carla E, Caraffa Alessandro, Ronconi Gianpaolo, Kritas Spyros K. IMpact of mast cells in fibromyalgia and low-grade chronic inflammation: Cen IL-37 play a role? Dermatological Therapy 2020 Jan;33(1):e13191. https://doi: 10.1111/dth.13191. Epub 2019 Dec 26.

33. Danilenko Olga V, Gavrilova Natalia Y, Churilov Leonid P. Chronic fatigue exhibits heterogeneous autoimmunity characteristics which reflect etiology. Pathophysiology 2022 May 25;29(2):187-199. https://doi: 10.3390/pathophysiology29020016.

34. Koniari Ioanna, Siminelakis Stavros N, Baikoussis Nikolaos G, Papadopoulos Georgios, Goudevenos John,

Apostolakis Efstratios. Antiphospholipid syndrome; its implication in cardiovascular disease: a review. Journal of Cardiothoracic Surgery 2010; 5: 101. Published online 2010 Nov 3. https://doi: 10.1186/1749-8090-5-101.

35. Dudek Jan. Role of cardiolipin in mitochondrial signaling pathways. Frontiers in Cell and Developmental Biology 2017; 5: 90. Published online 2017 Sep 29. https://doi: 10.3389/fcell.2017.00090.

36. Ikon Nikita, Ryan Robert O. Barth Syndrome: Connecting cardiolipin to cardiomyopathy. Lipids 2017 Feb; 52(2): 99-108. Published online 2017 Jan 9. https://doi: 10.1007/s11745-016-4229-7.

10. Chronic Fatigue Syndrome and the Cardiovascular System

1. Miwa Kunihisa, Fujita Masatoshi. Small heart syndrome in patients with chronic fatigue syndrome. Clinical Cardiology 2008 Jul;31(7):328-33. https://doi: 10.1002/clc.20227.

2. Staud Roland. Heart rate variability as a biomarker of fibromyalgia syndrome. Future Rheumatology 2008 Oct 1;3(5):475-483. https://doi: 10.2217/17460816.3.5.475.

3. van Campen C Linda MC, Verheugt Freek WA, Rowe Peter C, Visser Frans C. Cerebral blood flow is reduced in ME/CFS during head-up tilt testing even in the absence of hypotension or tachycardia: A quantitative, controlled study using Doppler Echography. Clinical Neurophysiological Practice 2020 Feb 8;5:50-58. https://doi: 10.1016/j.cnp.2020.01.003. eCollection 2020.

4. Benarroch Eduardo E. Postural tachycardia syndrome: A heterogeneous and multifactorial disorder. Mayo Clinic Proceedings 2012 Dec;87(12):1214-25. https://doi: 10.1016/j.mayocp.2012.08.013. Epub 2012 Nov 1.

5. Takizawa Peter. Vascular Endothelia. https://www.medcell.med.yale.edu, accessed 04/20/2022.

6. Feletou Michel. The endothelium: Part 1: Multiple functions of the endothelial cells—focus on endothelium-derived vasoactive mediators. In, Integrated Systems Physiology: from Molecule to Function to Disease (Editors: D. Neil Granger, Joey P. Granger). San Rafael, CA: Morgan & Claypool Life Sciences; 2011.

7. Medina-Leyte Diana J, Zepeda-Garcia Oscar, Dominguez-Perez Mayra, Gonzalez-Garrido Antonia, Villarreal-Molina Teresa, Jacobo-Albavera L. Endothelial dysfunction, inflammation and coronary artery disease: Potential biomarkers and promising therapeutical approaches. International Journal of Molecular Sciences 2021 2021 Apr 8;22(8):3850. https://doi: 10.3390/ijms22083850.

8. Daiber Andreas, Steven Sebastion, Weber Alina, et al. Targeting vascular (endothelial) dysfunction. British Journal of Pharmacology 2017 Jun;174(12):1591-1619. https://doi: 10.1111/bph.13517. Epub 2016 Jul 4.

9. Nawaz Iqra, Nawaz Yashfa, Nawaz Eisha, Manan Muhammad R, Mahmood Adil. Raynaud's Phenomenon: Reviewing the Pathophysiology and Management Strategies Cureus 2022 Jan 28;14(1):e21681. https://doi: 10.7759/cureus.21681. eCollection 2022 Jan.

10. Vaeroy Henning, Helle Robert, Forre Oystein, Kass Erik, Terenius Lars. Elevated CSF levels of substance P and high incidence of Raynaud phenomenon in patients with fibromyalgia: new features for diagnosis. Pain 1988 Jan;32(1):21-26. https://doi: 10.1016/0304-3959(88)90019-X.

11. Nietert Paul J, Shaftman Stephanie R, Silver Richard M, et al. Raynaud phenomenon and mortality: 20+ years of follow-up of the Charleston Heart Study cohort. Clinical Epidemiology 2015 Feb 3;7:161-8. https://doi: 10.2147/CLEP.S75482. eCollection 2015.

12. Arrais Rochas Eduardo, Mehta Niraj, Tavora-Mehta Maria ZP, Roncari Camila F, Cidrao Alan A, Neto Jorge E. Dysautonomia: A Forgotten Condition - Part 1. Arquivos Brasileiros de Cardiologia 2021 Apr;116(4):814-835. https://doi: 10.36660/abc.20200420.

13. Garner Richard, Baraniuk James N. Orthostatic intolerance in chronic fatigue syndrome. Journal of Translational Medicine 2019 Jun 3;17(1):185. https://doi: 10.1186/s12967-019-1935-y.

14. Van Campen C Linda MC, Rowe Peter C, Visser Frans C. Cerebral blood flow remains reduced after tilt testing in myalgic encephalomyelitis/chronic fatigue syndrome patients. Clinical Neurophysiology Practice 2021 Sep 23;6:245-255. https://doi: 10.1016/j.cnp.2021.09.001. eCollection 2021.

15. Sam. Living with Chronic Fatigue Syndrome. In, https:/ www. cfssamsite.wordpress.com, accessed 06/05/2022.

16. Steror Don. Extreme fatigue, brain fog, ringing in ears, head feels full. In, https://www. healthboards.com, accessed 06/05/2022.

17. Maksoud Rebekah D, du Preez Stanley, Eaton-Fitch Natalie, et al. A systematic review of neurological impairments in myalgic encephalomyelitis/chronic fatigue syndrome using neuroimaging techniques. PLoS ONE 2020 15(4): e0232475. https://doi.org/10.1371/ journal.pone.0232475.

18. Wirth Klaus J, Scheibenbogen Carmen, Paul Friedemann. An attempt to explain the neurological symptoms of Myalgic Encephalomyelitis/Chronic Fatigue Syndrome. Journal of Translational Medicine 2021 Nov 22;19(1):471. https://doi: 10.1186/s12967-021-03143-3.

19. Iliff Jeffrey J, Wang Minghuan, Liao Yonghong, et al. A paravascular pathway facilitates CSF flow through the brain parenchyma and the clearance of interstitial solutes, including

amyloid β. Science Translational Medicine 2012 Aug 15;4(147):147ra111. https://doi: 10.1126/scitranslmed.3003748.

20. Jessen Nadia A, Munk Anne SF, Lundgaard Iben, Nedergaard Maiken. The glymphatic system: A beginner's guide. Neurochemical Research 2015 Dec;40(12):2583-99. https://doi: 10.1007/s11064-015-1581-6. Epub 2015 May 7.

21. Chatterjee Kanu, Massie Barry. Systolic and diastolic heart failure: differences and similarities. Journal of Cardiac Failure 2007 Sep;13(7):569-76. https://doi: 10.1016/j.cardfail.2007.04.006.

22. Ramanlal Riddhi, Gupta Vikas. Physiology, Vasodilation. In: StatPearls [Internet]. Treasure Island, FL:StatPearls Publishing; 2022

23. Bozzini Sara, Albergati Andrea, Capelli Enrica, et al. Cardiovascular characteristics of chronic fatigue syndrome. Biomedical Reports 2018 Jan;8(1):26-30. https://doi: 10.3892/br.2017.1024. Epub 2017 Nov 28.

24. Haffke Milan, Freitag Helma, Rudolf Gordon, et al. Endothelial dysfunction and altered endothelial biomarkers in patients with post-COVID-19 syndrome and chronic fatigue syndrome (ME/CFS). Journal of Translational Medicine 2022 Mar 22;20(1):138. https://doi: 10.1186/s12967-022-03346-2.

25. Davenport Todd E, Lehnen Mary, Stevens Staci R, VanNess J. Mark, Stevens Jared, Snell Christopher R. Chronotropic intolerance: An overlooked determinant of symptoms and activity limitation in Myalgic Encephalomyelitis/Chronic Fatigue Syndrome? Frontiers in Pediatrics 2019 Mar 22;7:82. https://doi: 10.3389/fped.2019.00082. eCollection 2019.

26. Patel Seema, Rauf Abdur, Khan Haroon, Abu-Izneid Tareq. Renin-angiotensin-aldosterone (RAAS): The ubiquitous system for homeostasis and pathologies.

Biomedicine and Pharmacotherapy 2017 Oct;94:317-325. https://doi: 10.1016/j.biopha.2017.07.091. Epub 2017 Jul 31.

27. Wirth Klaus J, Scheibenbogen Carmen. Pathophysiology of skeletal muscle disturbances in myalgic encephalomyelitis/ chronic fatigue syndrome (ME/CFS). Journal of Translational Medicine 2021 Apr 21;19(1):162. https://doi: 10.1186/ s12967-021-02833-2.

28. Kubzansky Laura D, Adler Gail K. Aldosterone: a forgotten mediator of the relationship between psychological stress and heart disease. Neuroscience and Biobehavioral Reviews 2010 Jan;34(1):80-6. https://doi: 10.1016/ j.neubiorev.2009.07.005. Epub 2009 Jul 22.

29. Jason Leonard A., Corradi Karina, Gress Sara, Williams Sarah, Torres-Harding Susan. Causes of death among patients with chronic fatigue syndrome. Health Care for Women International 2006 Aug;27(7):615-26. https://doi: 10.1080/07399330600803766.

30. Roberts Emmert, Wessely Simon, Chalder Trudie, Chang Chin-Kuo, Hotopf Matthew. Mortality of people with chronic fatigue syndrome: a retrospective cohort study in England and Wales from the South London and Maudsley NHS Foundation Trust Biomedical Research Centre (SLaM BRC) Clinical Record Interactive Search (CRIS) Register. Lancet 2016 Apr 16;387(10028):1638-43. https://doi: 10.1016/ S0140-6736(15)01223-4. Epub 2016 Feb 10.

31. McManimen Stephanie L, Devendorf Andrew R, Brown Abigail A, Moore Billie C, Moore James H, Jason Leonard A. Mortality in patients with myalgic encephalomyelitis and chronic fatigue syndrome. Fatigue 2016;4(4):195-207.https:// doi: 10.1080/21641846.2016.1236588. Epub 2016 Oct 12.

32. Gist Anthea C, Guymer Emma K, Ajani Andrew E, Littlejohn Geoffrey O. Fibromyalgia has a high prevalence and impact in cardiac failure patients. European Journal of

Rheumatology 2017 Dec;4(4):245-249. doi: 10.5152/eurjrheum.2017.17026. Epub 2017 Nov 2.

11. Chronic Fatigue Syndrome and the Nervous System

1. Choy Ernest HS. The role of sleep in pain and fibromyalgia. Nature Reviews. Rheumatology 2015 Sep;11(9):513-20. https://doi: 10.1038/nrrheum.2015.56. Epub 2015 Apr 28.

2. Climent-Sanz Carolina, Morera-Amenós Genis, Bellon Filip et al. Poor sleep quality experience and self-management strategies in fibromyalgia: A qualitative metasynthesis. Journal of Clinical Medicine 2020 Dec 10;9(12):4000. https://doi: 10.3390/jcm9124000.

3. Mun Chung J, Davis Mary C, Campbell Claudia M, Finan Patrick H. Linking nonrestorative sleep and activity interference through pain catastrophizing and pain severity: An intraday process model among Individuals with Fibromyalgia. The Journal of Pain 2020 May-Jun;21(5-6):546-556. https://doi: 10.1016/j.jpain.2019.09.001. Epub 2019 Sep 14.

4. Bradley Laurence A. Pathophysiology of fibromyalgia. American Journal of Medicine 2009 Dec;122(12 Suppl):S22-30. https://doi: 10.1016/j.amjmed.2009.09.008.

5. Jackson Melinda L, Bruck Dorothy. Sleep abnormalities in chronic fatigue syndrome/myalgic encephalomyelitis: A review. Journal of Clinical Sleep Medicine 2012 Dec 15;8(6):719-28. https://doi: 10.5664/jcsm.2276.

6. Tanaka Masaaki, Tajima Seiki, Mizuno Kei, et al. Frontier studies on fatigue, autonomic nerve dysfunction, and sleep-rhythm disorder. The Journal of Physiological Sciences 2015 Nov;65(6):483-98. https://doi: 10.1007/s12576-015-0399-y. Epub 2015 Sep 29.

7. Morris Gerwyn, Berk Michael, Walder Ken, Maes Michael. Central pathways causing fatigue in neuroinflammatory and

autoimmune illnesses. BMC Medicine 2015 Feb 6;13:28. https://doi: 10.1186/s12916-014-0259-2.

8. Orjatsalo Maija, Alakuijala Anniina, Partinen. Autonomic nervous system functioning related to nocturnal sleep in patients with chronic fatigue syndrome compared to tired controls. Journal of Clinical Sleep Medicine 2018 Feb 15;14(2):163-171. doi: 10.5664/jcsm.6924.

9. Meadows Guy. The Sleep Book: How To Sleep Well Every Night. London, UK: Trade Paperback; 2014.

10. Milrad Sara F, Hall Daniel L, Jutagir Devika R, et al. Poor sleep quality is associated with greater circulating pro-inflammatory cytokines and severity and frequency of chronic fatigue syndrome/myalgic encephalomyelitis (CFS/ME) symptoms in women. Journal of Neuroimmunology 2017 Feb 15;303:43-50. https://doi: 10.1016/j.jneuroim.2016.12.008. Epub 2016 Dec 14.

11. Obal Jr Ferenc, Krueger James M. Biochemical regulation of non-rapid-eye-movement sleep. Frontiers in Bioscience 2003 May 1;8:d520-50. https://doi: 10.2741/1033.

12. Werbach Melvyn R. Nutritional strategies for treating chronic fatigue syndrome. Alternative Medicine Review 2000 Apr;5(2):93-108.

13. Parmeggiani Pier L. Thermoregulation and sleep. Frontiers in Bioscience 2003 May 1;8:s557-67. https://doi: 10.2741/1054.

14. Harding Edward C, Franks Nicholas P, Wisden William. The temperature dependence of sleep. Frontiers in Neuroscience 2019 Apr 24;13:336. https://doi: 10.3389/fnins.2019.00336.

15. Lack Leon C, Gradisar Michael, Van Someren Eus JW, Wright Helen R, Lushington Kurt. The relationship between

insomnia and body temperatures. Sleep Medicine Reviews 2008 Aug;12(4):307-17. https://doi: 10.1016/j.smrv.2008.02.003.

16. Morrrison Shaun F, Nakamura Kazuhiro. Central neural pathways for thermoregulation. Frontiers in Bioscience (landmark Edition) 2011 Jan 1;16(1):74-104. https://doi: 10.2741/3677.

17. Madden Christopher J, Morrison Shaun F. Central nervous system circuits that control body temperature. Neuroscience Letters 2019 Mar 23;696:225-232. https://doi: 10.1016/j.neulet.2018.11.027. Epub 2018 Dec 23.

18. Bollu Pradeep, Kaur Harleen. Sleep medicine: Insomnia and sleep. Missouri Medicine 2019 Jan-Feb; 116(1): 68–75.

19. Vethe Daniel, Kallestad Havard, Jaconsen Henrik B, Landro Nils I, Borchgrevink Petter C, Stiles Tore C. The relationship between improvement in insomnia severity and long-term outcomes in the treatment of chronic fatigue. Frontiers in Psychology 2018 Sep 21;9:1764. doi: 10.3389/fpsyg.2018.01764. eCollection 2018.

20. Ubeda-D'Ocasar Edurne, Diaz-Benito Victor J, Gallego-Sendarrubias Gracia M, Valera-Calero Juan A, Vicario-Merino A, Hervas-Perez Juan P. Pain and cortisol in patients with fibromyalgia: Systematic review and meta-analysis. Diagnostics (Basel) 2020 Nov 9;10(11):922. https://doi: 10.3390/diagnostics10110922.

21. Saconi Bruno, Polomano Rosemary C, Compton Peggy C, McPhillips Miranda V, Kuna Samuel T, Sawyer Amy M. The influence of sleep disturbances and sleep disorders on pain outcomes among veterans: A systematic scoping review. Sleep Medicine Reviews 2021 Apr;56:101411. https://doi: 10.1016/j.smrv.2020.101411. Epub 2020 Nov 30.

22. Whale Katie, Gooberman-Hill Rachael. The importance of sleep for people with chronic pain: Current insights and

evidence. JBMR Plus 2022 Jun 17;6(7):e10658. https://doi: 10.1002/jbm4.10658. eCollection 2022 Jul.

23. Smith Howard S, Harris Richard, Clauw Daniel. Fibromyalgia: an afferent processing disorder leading to a complex pain generalized syndrome. Pain Physician 2011 Mar-Apr;14(2):E217-45.

24. Lukkahatai Nada, Walitt Brian, Espina Alexandra, Gelio Alves, Saligan Leorey N. Understanding the association of fatigue with other symptoms of fibromyalgia: Development of a cluster model. Arthritis Care and Research 2016 Jan;68(1):99-107. https://doi: 10.1002/acr.22626.

25. Littlejohn Geoffrey, Guymer Emma. Neurogenic inflammation in fibromyalgia. Seminars in Immunopathology 2018 May;40(3):291-300. https://doi: 10.1007/s00281-018-0672-2. Epub 2018 Mar 19.

26. Nijs J, Lahousse A, Kapreli E, Bilika P, Saraçoğlu İ, et al. Nociplastic pain criteria or recognition of central sensitization? Pain phenotyping in the past, present, and future. Journal of Clinical Medicine 2021 Jul 21;10(15):3203. https://doi: 10.3390/jcm10153203.

27. Fitzcharles Mary-Ann, Cohen Steven P, Clauw Daniel J, Littlejohn Geoffrey, Usui Chie, Hauser Winifred. Nociplastic pain: Towards an understanding of prevalent pain conditions. Lancet 2021 May 29;397(10289):2098-2110. https://doi: 10.1016/S0140-6736(21)00392-5.

28. Pette Dirk, Staron Robert S. Myosin isoforms, muscle fiber types, and transitions. Microscopy Research and Technique 2000 Sep 15;50(6):500-9. https://doi: 10.1002/1097-0029(20000915)50:6<500::AID-JEMT7>3.0.CO;2-7.

29. Stuart Charles A, McCurry Melanie P, Marino A, et al. Slow-twitch fiber proportion in skeletal muscle correlates with insulin responsiveness. The Journal of Clinical Endocrinology

and Metabolism 2013 May;98(5):2027-36. https://doi: 10.1210/jc.2012-3876. Epub 2013 Mar 20.

30. Stump Craig S, Henriksen Erik J, Wei Yongzhong, Sowers James R. The metabolic syndrome: role of skeletal muscle metabolism. Annals of Medicine 2006;38(6):389-402. https://doi: 10.1080/07853890600888413.389-402.

31. El-Khoury Riyad, Bradford Aidan, O'Halloran Ken D. Chronic hypobaric hypoxia increases isolated rat fast-twitch and slow-twitch limb muscle force and fatigue. Physiological Research 2012;61(2):195-201. https://doi: 10.33549/physiolres.932140. Epub 2012 Jan 31.

32. Mense Siegfried. Muscle pain: mechanisms and clinical significance Deutsches Arzteblatt International 2008 Mar;105(12):214-9. doi: 10.3238/artzebl.2008.0214. Epub 2008 Mar 21.

33. Tomas Cara, Elson Joanna L, Newton Julia L, Walker Mark. Substrate utilisation of cultured skeletal muscle cells in patients with CFS. Scientific Reports 2020 Oct 26;10(1):18232. https://doi: 10.1038/s41598-020-75406-w.

34. Fernandez-Guerra Paula, Gonzalez-Ebsen Ana C, Boonen Susanne E, et al. Bioenergetic and proteomic profiling of immune cells in myalgic encephalomyelitis/chronic fatigue syndrome patients: An exploratory study. Biomolecules 2021 Jun 29;11(7):961. doi: 10.3390/biom11070961.

35. Maes Michael, Mihaylova Ivanka, Kubera Marta, Uytterhoeven Marc, Vrydags N, Bosmans Eugene. Coenzyme Q10 deficiency in myalgic encephalomyelitis/chronic fatigue syndrome (ME/CFS) is related to fatigue, autonomic and neurocognitive symptoms and is another risk factor explaining the early mortality in ME/CFS due to cardiovascular disorder. Neuro Endocrinology Letters 2009;30(4):470-6. PMID: 20010505.

36. Morris Gerwyn, Anderson George, Maes Michael. Hypothalamic-pituitary-adrenal hypofunction in myalgic encephalomyelitis (ME)/chronic fatigue syndrome (CFS) as a consequence of activated immune-inflammatory and oxidative and nitrosative pathways. Molecular Neurobiology 2017 Nov;54(9):6806-6819. https://doi: 10.1007/s12035-016-0170-2. Epub 2016 Oct 20.

37. Obata Hideaki. Analgesic mechanisms of antidepressants for neuropathic pain. International Journal of Molecular Sciences 2017 Nov 21;18(11):2483. https://doi: 10.3390/ijms18112483.

38 Janaszak-Jasiecka Anna, Siekierzycka Anna, Płoska Agata, Dobrucki Iwona T, Kalinowski Leszek. Endothelial dysfunction driven by hypoxia: The influence of oxygen deficiency on NO bioavailability. Biomolecules 2021 Jul 3;11(7):982. https://doi: 10.3390/biom11070982.

39. Lim Tony KY, Shi Xiang Q, Martin Hiliary C, et al. Blood-nerve barrier dysfunction contributes to the generation of neuropathic pain and allows targeting of injured nerves for pain relief. Pain 2014 May;155(5):954-967. https://doi: 10.1016/j.pain.2014.01.026. Epub 2014 Feb 3.

40. Wirth Klaus J, Scheibenbogen Carmen, Paul Friedemann. An attempt to explain the neurological symptoms of Myalgic Encephalomyelitis/Chronic Fatigue Syndrome. Journal of Translational Medicine 2021 Nov 22;19(1):471. https://doi: 10.1186/s12967-021-03143-3.

41. Pirahanchi Yasaman, Sharma Sandeep. Physiology, Bradykinin. In: StatPearls (Internet). Treasure Island, FL: StatPearls Publishing; 2021.

12. Chronic Fatigue Syndrome and Depression

1. Fitzcharles Mary-Ann, Cohen Steven P, Clauw Daniel J, Littlejohn Geoffrey, Usui Chie, Hauser Winifred. Nociplastic pain: Towards an understanding of prevalent pain conditions.

Lancet 2021 May 29;397(10289):2098-2110. https://doi: 10.1016/S0140-6736(21)00392-5.

2. Morris Gerwyn, Maes Michael, Berk Michael, Puri Basant K. Myalgic encephalomyelitis or chronic fatigue syndrome: how could the illness develop? Metabolic Brain Disease 2019 Apr;34(2):385-415. https://doi: 10.1007/s11011-019-0388-6. Epub 2019 Feb 13.

3. Wirth Klaus, Scheibenbogen Carmen. A Unifying Hypothesis of the Pathophysiology of Myalgic Encephalomyelitis/Chronic Fatigue Syndrome (ME/CFS): Recognitions from the finding of autoantibodies against ß2-adrenergic receptors. Autoimmunity Reviews 2020 Jun;19(6):102527. https://doi: 10.1016/j.autrev.2020.102527. Epub 2020 Apr 1.

4. Duque Laura, Fricchione Gregory. Fibromyalgia and its new lessons for neuropsychiatry. Medical Science Monitor Basic Science Research 2019 Jul 5;25:169-178. https://doi: 10.12659/MSMBR.915962.

5. Ben Simon E, Walker Matthew P. Underslept and overanxious: the neural correlates of sleep-loss induced anxiety in the human brain. Sleep Medicine December 2019 64:S31. https://doi: 10.1016/j.sleep.2019.11.086.

6. Jason Leonard A., Corradi Karina, Gress Sara, Williams Sarah, Torres-Harding Susan. Causes of death among patients with chronic fatigue syndrome. Health Care for Women International 2006 Aug;27(7):615-26. https://doi: 10.1080/07399330600803766.

7. Roberts Emmert, Wessely Simon, Chalder Trudie, Chang Chin-Kuo, Hotopf Matthew. Mortality of people with chronic fatigue syndrome: a retrospective cohort study in England and Wales from the South London and Maudsley NHS Foundation Trust Biomedical Research Centre (SLaM BRC) Clinical Record Interactive Search (CRIS) Register.

Lancet 2016 Apr 16;387(10028):1638-43. https://doi: 10.1016/S0140-6736(15)01223-4. Epub 2016 Feb 10.

8. McManimen Stephanie L, Devendorf Andrew R, Brown Abigail A, Moore Billie C, Moore James H, Jason Leonard A. Mortality in patients with myalgic encephalomyelitis and chronic fatigue syndrome. Fatigue 2016;4(4):195-207.https://doi: 10.1080/21641846.2016.1236588. Epub 2016 Oct 12.

9. Arrais Rochas Eduardo, Mehta Niraj, Tavora-Mehta Maria ZP, Roncari Camila F, Cidrao Alan A, Neto Jorge E. Dysautonomia: A forgotten condition - Part 1. Arquivos Brasileiros de Cardiologia 2021 Apr;116(4):814-835. https://doi: 10.36660/abc.20200420.

10. Maksoud Rebekah D, du Preez Stanley, Eaton-Fitc Natalie, et al. A systematic review of neurological impairments in myalgic encephalomyelitis/ chronic fatigue syndrome using neuroimaging techniques. PLoS ONE 2020 15(4): e0232475. https://doi.org/10.1371/ journal.pone.0232475.

11. Berardelli Isabella, Serafini Gianluca, Fiasche Federica, O'Connor Rory C, Pompili. The involvement of hypothalamus-pituitary-adrenal (HPA) axis in suicide risk. Brain Science 2020 Sep 21;10(9):653. https://doi: 10.3390/brainsci10090653.

12. Maes Michael, Twisk Frank. Why myalgic encephalomyelitis/chronic fatigue syndrome (ME/CFS) may kill you: disorders in the inflammatory and oxidative and nitrosative stress (IO&NS) pathways may explain cardiovascular disorders in ME/CFS. Neuro Endocrinology Letters 2009;30(6):677-93.

13. Maes Michael, Kubera Marta, Kotanska Magdalena. Aberrations in the cross-talks among redox, nuclear factor-κB, and wnt/β-catenin pathway signaling underpin myalgic encephalomyelitis and chronic fatigue syndrome. Frontiers in Psychiatry 2022 May 6;13:822382. https://doi: 10.3389/fpsyt.2022.822382. eCollection 2022.

14. Paul Bindu D, Lemle Marian D, Komaroff Anthony L, Snyder Solomon H. Redox imbalance links COVID-19 and myalgic encephalitis/chronic fatigue syndrome. Proceedings of the National Academy of Sciences of the USA 2021 Aug 24;118(34):e2024358118. https://doi: 10.1073/pnas.2024358118.

15. WHO. Depression, 09/13/21.https://www.who.int/news-room/fact-sheets/detail/depression, accessed 08/02/2022.

16. Celano Christopher, Villegas Ana C, Albanese Ariana M, Gaggin Hanna K, Huffman Jeff C. Depression and anxiety in heart failure: A review. Harvard Review of Psychiatry 2018 Jul/Aug;26(4):175-184. https://doi: 10.1097/HRP.0000000000000162.

17. Sbolli Marco, Fiuzat Mona, Cani Dario, O'Connor Christopher. Depression and heart failure: the lonely comorbidity. European Journal of Heart Failure 2020 Nov;22(11):2007-2017. https://doi: 10.1002/ejhf.1865. Epub 2020 May 29.

18. Dekker Rebecca L. Patient perspectives about depressive symptoms in heart failure: A review of the qualitative literature. Journal of Cardiovascular Nursing 2014 Jan-Feb;29(1):E9-15. https://doi: 10.1097/JCN.0b013e318273a5d6.

19. Smolderen Kim G, Buchanan Donna M, Gosch Kensey, et al. Depression treatment and 1-year mortality after acute myocardial infarction: Insights from the TRIUMPH registry (Translational Research Investigating Underlying Disparities in Acute Myocardial Infarction Patients' Health Status). Circulation 2017 May 2;135(18):1681-1689. https://doi: 10.1161/CIRCULATIONAHA.116.025140. Epub 2017 Feb 16.

20. Harshfield Eric L, Pennells Lisa, Schwartz Joseph E, et al. Association between depressive symptoms and incident cardiovascular diseases. Journal of the American Medical Association 2020 Dec 15;324(23):2396-2405. https://doi: 10.1001/jama.2020.23068.2020 Dec 15;324(23):2396-2405.

21. Heo Seongkum, Moser Debra K, Pressler Susan J, et al. Dose-dependent relationship of physical and depressive symptoms with health-related quality of life in patients with heart failure. European Journal of Cardiovascular Nursing 2013 Oct;12(5):454-60. https://doi: 10.1177/1474515112470996. Epub 2013 Jan 2.

22. Dantzer Robert, O'Connor Jason C, Freund Gregory C, Johnson Rodney W, Kelley Keith W. From inflammation to sickness and depression: when the immune system subjugates the brain. Nature Reviews Neuroscience 2008 Jan;9(1):46-56. https://doi: 10.1038/nrn2297.

23. Armour J. Andrew, Ardell Jeffrey L.. Basic and Clinical Neurocardiology. New York, NY: Oxford University Press; 2004.

24. Thayer Julian F, Yamamoto Shelby S, Brosschot Jos F. The relationship of autonomic imbalance, heart rate variability and cardiovascular disease risk factors. International Journal of Cardiology 2010 May 28;141(2):122-31. https://doi: 10.1016/j.ijcard.2009.09.543. Epub 2009 Nov 11.

25. Patel Jay S, Bernston Jessica, Polanka Brittany M, Stewart Jesse C. Cardiovascular risk factors as differential predictors of incident atypical and typical major depressive disorder in US adults. Psychosomatic Medicine 2018 Jul/Aug;80(6):508-514. https://doi: 10.1097/PSY.0000000000000583.

26. Zhou Siyao, Zhao Ke, Shi Xiang, et al. Serum lipid levels and suicide attempts within 2 weeks in patients with major depressive disorder: Is there a relationship? Frontiers in Psychiatry 2021 Jun 7;12:676040. doi: 10.3389/fpsyt.2021.676040. eCollection 2021.

27. Wilson Marlene A, Liberzon Israel, Lindsey Merry L, et al. Common pathways and communication between the brain and heart: connecting post-traumatic stress disorder and heart

failure. Stress 2019 Sep;22(5):530-547. https://doi: 10.1080/10253890.2019.1621283. Epub 2019 Jun 4.

28. Xu Chengyang, Tao Xueshu, Ma Xiaonan, Zhao Rui, Cao Zhipeng. Cognitive dysfunction after heart disease: A manifestation of the heart-brain axis. Oxidative Medicine and Cellular Longevity 2021 Aug 18;2021:4899688. https://doi: 10.1155/2021/4899688. eCollection 2021.

29. Nagai Michiaki, Förster Carola Y, Dote Keigo. Sex hormone-specific neuroanatomy of Takotsubo syndrome: Is the insular cortex a moderator? Biomolecules 2022 Jan 10;12(1):110. https://doi: 10.3390/biom12010110.

30. Nagai Michiaki, Dote Keigo, Kato Masaya, et al. The insular cortex and Takotsubo cardiomyopathy. Current Pharmaceutical Design 2017;23(6):879-888. doi: 10.2174/1381612822666161006123530.

31. Ichesco Eric, Schmidt-Wilcke Tobias, Bhavsar Rupal, et al. Altered resting state connectivity of the insular cortex in individuals with fibromyalgia. The Journal of Pain 2014 Aug;15(8):815-826.e1. doi: 10.1016/j.jpain.2014.04.007. Epub 2014 May 9.

32. Wortinger Laura A, Oie Merete G, Endestad Tor, Wylle Vegard B. Altered right anterior insular connectivity and loss of associated functions in adolescent chronic fatigue syndrome. PLoS One 2017 Sep 7;12(9):e0184325. https://doi: 10.1371/journal.pone.0184325. eCollection 2017.

33. Zou Rongjun, Shi Wanting, Tao Jun, et al. Neurocardiology: Cardiovascular changes and specific brain region infarcts. BioMed Research International 2017;2017:5646348. https://doi: 10.1155/2017/5646348. Epub 2017 Jul 3.

34. Cengic Sabina, Zuberi Muhammad, Bansal Vikas, Ratzlaff, Rodrigues Eduardo, Festic Emir. Hypotension after intensive care unit drop-off in adult cardiac surgery patients.

World Journal of Critical Care Medicine 2020 Jun 5;9(2):20-30. https://doi: 10.5492/wjccm.v9.i2.20.

35. Hori Daijiro, Ono Masahiro, Rappold Thomas E, et al. Hypotension After cardiac operations based on autoregulation monitoring leads to brain cellular injury. The Annals of Thoracic Surgery 2015 Aug;100(2):487-93. https://doi: 10.1016/j.athoracsur.2015.03.036. Epub 2015 Jun 16.

36. Neumann Inga D, Landgraf Rainer. Balance of brain oxytocin and vasopressin: implications for anxiety, depression, and social behaviors. Trends in Neurosciences 2012 Nov;35(11):649-59. https://doi: 10.1016/j.tins.2012.08.004. Epub 2012 Sep 11.

37. De Melo Leonardo A, Almeida-Santos Ana F. Neuropsychiatric properties of the ACE2/Ang-(1-7)/Mas pathway: A brief review. Protein and Peptide Letters 2020;27(6):476-483. https://doi: 10.2174/0929866527666191223143230.

38. Dantzer Robert, O'Connor Jason C, Lawson Marcus A, Kelley Keith W. Inflammation-Associated Depression: From Serotonin to Kynurenine. Psychoneuroendocrinology 2011 Apr;36(3):426-36. doi: 10.1016/j.psyneuen.2010.09.012. Epub 2010 Oct 30.

39. Toledo Camilo, Andrade David, Diaz Hugo S, Inestrosa Nibaldo C, Del Rio Rodrigo. Neurocognitive disorders in heart failure: Novel pathophysiological mechanisms underpinning memory loss and learning impairment. Molecular Neurobiology 2019 Dec;56(12):8035-8051. https://doi: 10.1007/s12035-019-01655-0. Epub 2019 Jun 5.

40. Neto Emidio B, de Freitas Lucas A, Pimenta Daniel C, Lebrun Ivo, Nencioni Ana L. Tb1, a neurotoxin from Tityus bahiensis scorpion venom, induces epileptic seizures by increasing glutamate release. Toxins 2020 Jan 21;12(2):65. https://doi: 10.3390/toxins12020065.

41. Corriger Alexandrine, Pickering Gisele. Ketamine and depression: a narrative review. Drug Design, Development and Therapy 2019 Aug 27;13:3051-3067. https://doi: 10.2147/DDDT.S221437. eCollection 2019.

42. Sanders Owen. Sildenafil for the treatment of Alzheimer's disease: A systematic review. Journal of Alzheimer's Disease Reports 2020 Apr 22;4(1):91-106. https://doi: 10.3233/ADR-200166.

43. Olimulder Marion AGM, Galjee Michel A, Wagenaar Lodewijk J, et al. Chronic fatigue syndrome in women assessed with combined cardiac magnetic resonance imaging. Netherlands Heart Journal 2016 Dec;24(12):709-716. https://doi: 10.1007/s12471-016-0885-8.

44. Hollingsworth Kieren G, Hodgson Tim, MacGowan Guy A, Blamire Andrew M, Newton Julia L. Impaired cardiac function in chronic fatigue syndrome measured using magnetic resonance cardiac tagging. Journal of Internal Medicine 2012 Mar;271(3):264-70. https://doi: 10.1111/j.1365-2796.2011.02429.x. Epub 2011 Aug 15.

45. Bowles Neil E, Bayston Trevor A, Zhang Hongyi, et al. Persistence of enterovirus RNA in muscle biopsy samples suggests that some cases of chronic fatigue syndrome result from a previous, inflammatory viral myopathy. Journal of Medicine 1993;24(2-3):145-60.

46. Ritterhoff Julia, Tian Rong. Metabolism in cardiomyopathy: Every substrate matters. Cardiovascular Research 2017 Mar 15;113(4):411-421. https://doi: 10.1093/cvr/cvx017.

47. Zhou Bo, Tian Rong. Mitochondrial dysfunction in pathophysiology of heart failure. The Journal of Clinical Investigation 2018 Aug 31;128(9):3716-3726. https://doi: 10.1172/JCI120849. Epub 2018 Aug 20.

48. Beuchel Carl, Dittrich Julia, Pott Janne, et al. Blood metabolite profiles reflect changes in energy metabolism in heart failure. Metabolites 2022 Feb 27;12(3):216. https://doi: 10.3390/metabo12030216.

49. Chouchou Florian, Mauguiere Francois, Vallayer Ophelie, et al. How the insula speaks to the heart: Cardiac responses to insular stimulation in humans. Human Brain Mapping 2019 Jun 15;40(9):2611-2622. https://doi: 10.1002/hbm.24548. Epub 2019 Feb 28.

13. Promising Treatment Approaches

1. Bustamante-Sánchez Álvaro, Tornero-Aguilera José F, Fernández-Elías Valentín E, et al. Effect of stress on autonomic and cardiovascular systems in military population: A systematic review. Cardiology Research and Practice 2020 Aug 11;2020:7986249. https://doi: 10.1155/2020/7986249.

2. Arrais Rochas Eduardo, Mehta Niraj, Tavora-Mehta Maria ZP, Roncari Camila F, Cidrao Alan A, Neto Jorge E. Dysautonomia: A forgotten condition - Part 1. Arquivos Brasileiros de Cardiologia 2021 Apr;116(4):814-835. https://doi: 10.36660/abc.20200420.

3. Carrara Marta, Ferrario Manuela, Bollen Pinto Bernardo, Herpain Antoine. The autonomic nervous system in septic shock and its role as a future therapeutic target: a narrative review. Annals of Intensive Care 2021 May 17;11(1):80. https:// doi: 10.1186/s13613-021-00869-7.

4. Spallone Vincenza. Update on the impact, diagnosis and management of cardiovascular autonomic neuropathy in diabetes: What is defined, what is new, and what is unmet. Diabetes Metabolism Journal 2019 Feb; 43(1): 3–30. https:// doi:10.4093/dmj.2018.0259.

5. McCraty Rollin. New! Science of the Heart: Exploring the Role of the Heart in Human Performance. Boulder Creek, CA: HeartMath Institute; 2016. Ebook at https://

www.heartmath.org/research/science-of-the-heart/, accessed 09/14/2022.

6. Elbers Jorina, McCraty Rollin. HeartMath approach to self-regulation and psychosocial well-being. Journal of Psychology in Africa 2020 30:1, 69-79. https://doi:10.1080/14330237.2020.1712797.

7. Armour J Andrew. Potential clinical relevance of the 'little brain' on the mammalian heart. Experimental Physiology 2007 93(2), 165–176. https://doi.org/10.1113/ expphysiol.2007 .041178.

8. Lloyd Anthony, Brett David, Wesnes Keith. Coherence training in children with attention-deficit hyperactivity disorder: Cognitive functions and behavioural changes. Alternative Therapies in Health and Medicine 2010 16(4), 34–42. PMID: 20653294.

9. Berry Melanie, Chapple Iva T, Ginsberg Jay P, Gleichauf Kurt J, Meyer Jeff A, Nagpal Madan L. Non-pharmacological intervention for chronic pain in veterans: A pilot study of heart rate variability biofeedback. Global Advances in Health and Medicine: Improving Healthcare Outcomes Worldwide 2014 3(2), 28–33. https://doi.org/10.7453/gahmj.2013.075 PMID: 24808979.

10. Ginsberg Jay P, Berry Melanie E, Powell Donald A. Cardiac coherence and posttraumatic stress disorder in combat veterans. Alternative Therapies in Health and Medicine 2010 16(4), 52–60. PMID: 20653296.

11. McCraty Rollin, Atkinson Mike. Resilience training program reduces physiological and psychological stress in police officers. Global Advances in Health and Medicine: Improving Healthcare Outcomes Worldwide 2012 1(5), 44–66. https://doi.org/10.7453/gahmj.2012.1.5.013.

12. Li Wen-Chin, Chiu Fa-Chung, Kuo Ying-Shin, Wu Ka-Jay. The investigation of visual attention and workload by experts and novices in the cockpit. In D. Harris (Ed.),

Engineering Psychology and Cognitive Ergonomics. Applications and Services, 167–176. Heidelberg, Germany: Springer; 2013. https://doi .org/10.1007/978-3-642-39354-9_19.

13. McCraty Rollin, Atkinson Mike, Lipsenthal Lee, Arguelles Lourdes. New hope for correctional officers: An innovative program for reducing stress and health risks. Applied Psychophysiology and Biofeedback 2009 34(4), 251–272. https:// doi.org/10.1007/s10484-009-9087-0.

14. Cruz Marina Z, de Godoy Moacir F, Valenti Vitor E, Pereira Jr Alfredo, Cardoso Roberto AD. The effects of slow breathing exercise on heart rate dynamics and cardiorespiratory coherence in preschool children: A prospective clinical study. Alternative Therapies in Health and Medicine 2020 Jul;26(4):14-21.

15. Alabdulgader Abdullah A. Coherence: A novel nonpharmacological modality for lowering blood pressure in hypertensive patients. Global Advances in Health and Medicine 2012 May;1(2):56-64. https://doi: 10.7453/gahmj.2012.1.2.011.

16. Luskin Frederic, Reitz Megan, Newell Kathryn, Quinn Thomas G, Haskell William. A controlled pilot study of stress management training of elderly patients with congestive heart failure. Preventive Cardiology 2002 Fall;5(4):168-72. doi: 10.1111/j.1520.037X.2002.01029.x.

17. Burch James, Ginsberg Jay P, McLain Alexander C, et al. Symptom management among cancer survivors: Randomized pilot intervention trial of heart rate variability biofeedback. Applied Psychophysiology and Biofeedback 2020 Jun;45(2):99-108. https://doi: 10.1007/s10484-020-09462-3.

18. Anasuya Boligarla, Deepak Kishore K, Jaryal Ashok K. Autonomic tone and baroreflex sensitivity during 70° head-up tilt in yoga practitioners. International Journal of Yoga 2020 Sep-Dec;13(3):200-206. https://doi: 10.4103/ijoy.IJOY_29_20. Epub 2020 Sep 13.

19. Lipov Eugene, Lipov Sergei, Stark Jamie T. Stellate ganglion blockade provides relief from menopausal hot flashes: A case report series. Journal of Women's Health 2005 2005 Oct;14(8):737-41. https://doi: 10.1089/jwh.2005.14.737.

20. Liao Chun-De, Tsauo Jau-Yih, Liou Tsan-Hon, Chen Hung-Chou, Rau Chi-Lun. Efficacy of noninvasive stellate ganglion blockade performed using physical agent modalities in patients with sympathetic hyperactivity-associated disorders: A systematic review and meta-analysis. PLoS One 20162;11(12):e0167476. https://doi: 10.1371/journal.pone.0167476.

21. Ganesh Arun, Qadri Yarwa J, Boortz-Marx Richard L, et al. Stellate ganglion blockade: An intervention for the management of ventricular arrhythmias. Current Hypertension Reports 2020 Oct 23;22(12):100. https://doi: 10.1007/s11906-020-01111-8.

22. Mulvaney Sean W, Lynch James H, Hickey Matthew J, et al. Stellate ganglion block used to treat symptoms associated with combat-related post-traumatic stress disorder: A case series of 166 patients. Military Medicine 2014 179(10),1133–1140, https://doi.org/10.7205/MILMED-D-14-00151.

23. Lipov Eugene G, Jacobs Ryan, Springer Shauna, Candido Kenneth D, Knezevic Nebojsa N. Utility of cervical sympathetic block in treating post-traumatic stress disorder in multiple cohorts: A retrospective analysis. Pain Physician 2022 Jan;25(1):77-85. PMID: 35051147.

24. Sahin Omer F, Kilic Ebru T, Aksoy Yakup, Kaydu Ayhan, Gokcek Erhan. The importance of perfusion index monitoring in evaluating the efficacy of stellate ganglion blockage treatment in Raynaud's disease. Libyan Journal of Medicine 2018 Jan 19. https://doi:10.1080/19932820.2017.1422666.

25. Lipov Eugene G, Candido Kenneth, Richies Elspeth C. Possible reversal of PTSD-related DNA methylation by

sympathetic blockade. Journal of Molecular Neuroscience 2017 May;62(1):67-72. https://doi: 10.1007/s12031-017-0911-3. Epub 2017 Mar 31.

26. Melkani Girish C, Panda Satchidananda T. Time-restricted feeding for prevention and treatment of cardiometabolic disorders. The Journal of Physiology 2017 Jun 15;595(12):3691-3700. https://doi: 10.1113/JP273094. Epub 2017 Apr 25.

27. Longo Valter D, Antebi Adam, Bartke Andrzej, et al. Interventions to slow aging in humans: Are we ready? Aging Cell 2015 Aug;14(4):497-510. https://doi: 10.1111/acel.12338. Epub 2015 Apr 22.

28. Patikorn Chanthawat, Roubal Kiera, Veettil Sajesh K, et al. Intermittent fasting and obesity-related health outcomes: An umbrella review of meta-analyses of randomized clinical trials. JAMA Network Open 2021 Dec 1;4(12):e2139558. https://doi: 10.1001/jamanetworkopen.2021.39558.

29. Schroder Jessica D, Falqueto Hugo, Manica Alina et al. Effects of time-restricted feeding in weight loss, metabolic syndrome and cardiovascular risk in obese women. Journal of Translational Medicine 2021 Jan 6;19(1):3. https:// doi: 10.1186/s12967-020-02687-0.

30. Wahls Terry L. Minding My Mitochondria: How I Overcame Secondary Progressive Multiple Sclerosis (MS) and Got Out of My Wheelchair. Iowa City, IA: TZ press, LLC; 2010.

31. Benedetti Francesco, Colombo Cristina. Sleep deprivation in mood disorders. Neuropsychobiology 2011;64(3):141-51. https://doi: 10.1159/000328947. Epub 2011 Jul 29.

32. Benedetti Francesco, Dallaspezia Sara, Melloni Elisa MT, et al. Effective antidepressant chronotherapeutics (sleep deprivation and light therapy) normalize the IL-1β:IL-1ra ratio

in bipolar depression. Frontiers in Physiology 2021 Sep 1;12:740686. doi: 10.3389/fphys.2021.740686. eCollection 2021.

33. Levitan Robert D. The chronobiology and neurobiology of winter seasonal affective disorder. Dialogues in Clinical Neuroscience 2007;9(3):315-24. https://doi: 10.31887/DCNS.2007.9.3/rlevitan.

34. Chen Nan, Wu Quan, Xiong Yanlei, Chen Guang, Song Dandan, Xu Chengli. Circadian rhythm and sleep during prolonged Antarctic residence at Chinese Zhongshan Station. Wilderness and Environmental Medicine 2016 Dec;27(4):458-467. https://doi: 10.1016/j.wem.2016.07.004.

35. Arendt Josephine. Biological rhythms during residence in polar regions. Chronobiology International 2012 May;29(4):379-94. https://doi: 10.3109/07420528.2012.668997. Epub 2012 Apr 12.

36. Arendt Josephine, Middleton B. Human seasonal and circadian studies in Antarctica (Halley, 75°S). General and Comparative Endocrinology 2018 Mar 1;258:250-258. https://doi: 10.1016/j.ygcen.2017.05.010. Epub 2017 May 17.

15. Conclusion

1. Zou Rongjun, Shi Wanting, Tao Jun, et al. Neurocardiology: Cardiovascular changes and specific brain region infarcts. BioMed Research International 2017;2017:5646348. https://doi: 10.1155/2017/5646348. Epub 2017 Jul 3.

2. Xu Chengyang, Tao Xueshu, Ma Xiaonan, Zhao Rui, Cao Zhipeng. Cognitive Dysfunction after Heart Disease: A Manifestation of the Heart-Brain Axis. Oxidative Medicine and Cellular Longevity 2021 Aug 18;2021:4899688. https://doi: 10.1155/2021/4899688. eCollection 2021.

3. Arrais Rochas Eduardo, Mehta Niraj, Tavora-Mehta Maria ZP, Roncari Camila F, Cidrao Alan A, Neto Jorge E.

Dysautonomia: A Forgotten Condition - Part 1. Arquivos Brasileiros de Cardiologia 2021 Apr;116(4):814-835. https://doi: 10.36660/abc.20200420.

4. van Campen C Linda MC, Verheugt Freek WA, Rowe Peter C, Visser Frans C. Cerebral blood flow is reduced in ME/CFS during head-up tilt testing even in the absence of hypotension or tachycardia: A quantitative, controlled study using Doppler Echography. Clinical Neurophysiological Practice 2020 Feb 8;5:50-58. https://doi: 10.1016/j.cnp.2020.01.003. eCollection 2020.

5. Ritterhoff Julia, Tian Rong. Metabolism in cardiomyopathy: Every substrate matters. Cardiovascular Research 2017 Mar 15;113(4):411-421. https://doi: 10.1093/cvr/cvx017.

6. Ghali Alaa, Lacout Carole, Ghali Maria, et al. Elevated blood lactate in resting conditions correlate with post-exertional malaise severity in patients with myalgic encephalomyelitis/chronic fatigue syndrome. Scientific Reports 2019 Dec 11;9(1):18817. https://doi: 10.1038/s41598-019-55473-4.

7. Castro-Diehl Cecilia, Diez Roux Ana V, Redline Susan, et al. Sleep Duration and Quality in Relation to Autonomic Nervous System Measures: The Multi-Ethnic Study of Atherosclerosis (MESA). Sleep 2016 Nov 1; 39(11): 1927–1940. https://doi: 10.5665/sleep.6218.

8. Parmeggiani Pier L. Thermoregulation and sleep. Frontiers in Bioscience 2003 May 1;8:s557-67. https://doi: 10.2741/1054.

9. Harding Edward C, Franks Nicholas P, Wisden William. The temperature dependence of sleep. Frontiers in Neuroscience 2019 Apr 24;13:336. https://doi: 10.3389/fnins.2019.00336.

10. Jackson Melinda L, Bruck Dorothy. Sleep abnormalities in chronic fatigue syndrome/myalgic encephalomyelitis: A review.

Journal of Clinical Sleep Medicine 2012 Dec 15;8(6):719-28. https://doi: 10.5664/jcsm.2276.

11. Danilenko Olga V, Gavrilova Natalia Y, Churilov Leonid P. Chronic fatigue exhibits heterogeneous autoimmunity characteristics which reflect etiology. Pathophysiology 2022 May 25;29(2):187-199. https://doi: 10.3390/pathophysiology29020016.

12. Reardon Colin, Murray Kaitlin, Lomax Alan E. Neuroimmune communication in health and disease. Physiological Reviews 2018 Oct 1;98(4):2287-2316. https://doi: 10.1152/physrev.00035.2017.

13. Meadows Guy. The Sleep Book: How to Sleep Well Every Night. London, UK:The Sleep School; 2014.

14. McCraty Rollin. New! Science of the Heart: Exploring the Role of the Heart in Human Performance. Boulder Creek, CA: HeartMath Institute; 2016. Ebook at https://www.heartmath.org/research/science-of-the-heart/,accessed 09/14/2022.

Acknowledgment

I thank Hannah Schandelmeier-Lynch for her support and advice, and for helping to bring this book to the market.

www.ingramcontent.com/pod-product-compliance
Lightning Source LLC
LaVergne TN
LVHW090312210926
848480LV00001B/225
9798987117712